The Great Hanging at Gainesville, 1862

The Great Hanging at Gainesville, 1862

The Accounts of Thomas Barrett and George Washington Diamond

Introduction by Richard B. McCaslin

Afterword By L. D. Clark

Texas State Historical Association
Denton

The great hanging at Gainesville, 1862: the accounts of Thomas Barrett and George Washington Diamond/by Thomas Barrett and George Washington Diamond; introduction by Richard B. McCaslin; afterword by L. D. Clark.
182 p.
Editor's note by Ryan R. Schumacher.
Barrett's account originally published under the title: The great hanging at Gainesville, Cooke County, Texas, October, A.D. 1862. Gainesville, Tex.: [s.n.], 1885 and republished in Austin, Tex. by the Texas State Historical Association, 1961. Diamond's account originally prepared in manuscript form ca. 1874–1876; first book publication: Account of the great hanging at Gainesville, 1862. Austin: Texas State Historical Association, 1963.
SBN 978-0-87611-255-7 — ISBN 0-87611-255-6 1. Hanging–Texas–Gainesville--History–19th century. 2. Gainesville (Tex.)–History–19th century. 3. Texas–History–Civil War, 1861–1865. I. McCaslin, Richard B. II. Schumacher, Ryan R. III. Acheson, Sam Hanna, 1900–1972. IV. O'Connell, Julie Ann Hudson. V. Barrett, Thomas, 1809–1892. Great hanging at Gainesville, Cooke County, Texas, October, A.D. 1862. VI. Diamond, George Washington, 1835–1911. Account of the great hanging at Gainesville, 1862. VII. Title: Great hanging at Gainesville. VIII. Title: George Washington Diamond's account of the great hanging at Gainesville, 1862.

Contents

Editor's Note

The Texas State Historical Association (TSHA) is pleased to offer a new publication of two accounts of one of the most controversial events in our state's history, the 1862 Great Hanging at Gainesville. The accounts by Thomas Barrett (1885) and George Washington Diamond (1874–76?)—strikingly different in their interpretations--are the only known narratives written by individuals personally connected to the Great Hanging. Barrett himself served on the "Citizens Court" that tried the men hanged, while Diamond's brother James J. Diamond was one of the organizers of the court. Published separately by the TSHA in the early 1960s and long out of print, we now offer them with a new introduction by Richard B. McCaslin, a noted historian of nineteenth-century Texas and the Civil War, and an afterword by L. D. Clark, a descendent of one of the men hanged who shows that even after 150 years, passions still run high. Barrett's account was first published as a book in 1961; Diamond's account first appeared, with annotations by Sam Acheson and Julie Ann Hudson O'Connell, as an article in the January 1963 issue of the *Southwestern Historical Quarterly* (Vol. 66, No. 3) and was published a book later that year. We have published Barrett's and Diamond's account exactly as they were upon the 1960s publication, including typos and misspellings, except for an index to Diamond's account. The annotations of Diamond's account have been preserved.

Ryan R. Schumacher
Texas State Historical Association

Introduction

By Richard B. McCaslin

Texans do not treasure all of their memories. In fact, many prefer not to remember some events in Texas history at all. One such affair is the Great Hanging at Gainesville, which took place in October 1862. After an initial flurry of newspaper reports, participants simply stopped talking about what had happened, and most of the new residents who flooded into North Texas after the Civil War had little interest in the matter and even less knowledge of it. The latter, many of whom had served in the Confederate military or who had relatives and friends who did, raised a monument to the Confederacy in Gainesville with an inscription that read in part, "No Nation Rose So White and Fair; None Fell So Free of Crime." While this may have reflected their own experiences in the embattled South or what they wanted to remember, it seemed to others to be supremely ironic that this edifice stood a short distance from where forty men had been hanged by a vigilante court for allegedly opposing the Confederacy.

It was not until almost a century after the Great Hanging that an eyewitness account was published by the Texas State Historical Association (TSHA). Written by Thomas Barrett and first printed in 1885, only three copies existed at the time of its republication in 1961. The association then published another primary source in 1963. Edited by Sam Acheson and Julia Ann H. O'Connell, it had supposedly been compiled from the original records of the vigilante court by George W. Diamond, a younger brother of two men who were marginally involved in the Great Hanging.

This led to the appearance of a few articles in historical magazines written by Philip Rutherford and James Smallwood and the memoir of James Lemuel Clark, son of one of the men hanged at Gainesville. Not until 1994 did my book, *Tainted Breeze,* appear. In this work, I used the Barrett's recollections, Diamond's fragmented records, Clark's memoir, as well as many other sources to retrieve the history of the Great Hanging from the dim recesses of popular memory to which it had been consigned. I have used *Tainted Breeze* to provide the material, including the quotations, for this introduction to a second, combined edition of Barrett's and Diamond's accounts.

Why resurrect the Great Hanging at all? Because if Texans and Americans are to understand the Civil War and its impact fully, they need to strip away the cobwebs of popular memory and confront the actual history of that horrific national conflict. The Civil War fractured families both on the battlefield and on the home front, where Americans north and south clashed over resources and security as much as ideologies. Every Confederate state had dissenters, and violence was often used against them. This proved to be especially true in Texas, where frontier conditions enhanced concerns for resources and security. Furthermore, the lack of established legal agencies led many settlers to resort to vigilantism when faced with danger. When effective action was taken against outsiders, such as raiding Indians or plundering outlaws, then the grim accomplishments of a community and its leaders often became the source of proud stories to be retold and even published. But when the targets were members of the community, victims of a temporary allegiance to a failed rebellion, then the tales were not told. Barrett found it almost impossible to market his testimony, and Diamond did not have his manuscript printed at all. The actual vigilante court records disappeared because no one cared to save them. Instead, a myth of southern infallibility and unity replaced a simple truth, which is that Confederates were just as prone to mistakes and just as contentious as any embattled people. Sadly, the effects of their struggle shaped regional and national history in ways that many people would rather not contemplate. The origins of the Great Hanging lie deep in the history of North Texas. Gainesville is the seat of Cooke County, which sits within the watersheds of the Trinity and Red Rivers. Early settlement proceeded slowly until the arrival of the Butterfield Overland Mail route in 1858. The stage line entered Texas across the Red River and crossed Grayson into Cooke County before passing through Gainesville. Settlers followed it in droves. The population of Cooke County in 1850 was 220; by 1860, it became 3,760. An Army officer in 1854 described Gainesville as a "collection of five or six log cabins, dignified with the name of a town." In 1859, a later visitor saw fifty or sixty houses, "most of them neat edifices and none shabby." The 1860 census listed 280 people in the town, which the *Texas Almanac* asserted was "perhaps one of the most pleasant . . . in North Texas." It boasted two hotels, a frame courthouse that also served as a school, and the only post office in the county.

This flood of immigrants created sharp divisions that mirrored those in Texas, and the South, as a whole. By 1860, non-slaveholders from the Upper South remained a majority in Cooke County, but a slave owner minority, mostly from the Lower South, dominated the local economy. As elsewhere, economic prominence became political dominance. In 1861 the chief justice, sheriff, and three of four county commissioners owned slaves. Local slaveholders also led volunteers against Indians, especially the Comanche, who evaded the federal troops on the frontier. James G. Bourland commanded a company of volunteers in 1858, and his brother led a similar unit in Grayson County. Their targets were not always Indians. Four white raiders in Jack County, carved from Cooke in 1856, were hanged by vigilantes. Bourland's brother killed two slaves in an insurrection allegedly inspired by abolitionists. Too, Bourland's son-in-law, slave owner Samuel C. Doss, chaired a Gainesville meeting that exiled an accused abolitionist.

Unfortunately for those concerned with order and security, more abolitionists soon came. Ministers of the Northern Methodist Episcopal Church refused to accept the schism over slavery in their church and continued to preach in areas claimed by southern preachers. Dallas vigilantes in 1858 whipped and exiled two Northern Methodist ministers. John Brown's raid on Harper's Ferry greatly increased tensions. Tempers flared when fires erupted in July 1860, damaging property in Gainesville and other North Texas communities. Some insisted that the summer heat had ignited phosphorous matches in local stores, but most believed the fires were an abolitionist attack. On July 28, 1860, John Marshall of the Austin *Texas State Gazette* printed a note from Charles R. Pryor of the *Dallas Herald*, who opined that the fires were evidence of a "deep laid scheme of villainy to devastate the whole of Northern Texas." Many fled North Texas after the fires, but vigilantes found several victims. William H. Crawford was lynched at Fort Worth. Methodist elder Anthony Bewley was chased to Missouri, returned to North Texas, and hanged. Nearly one hundred slaves were arrested in Dallas; three were lynched, while the others were whipped. Emotions were inflamed by rumors of abolitionist activity that increased with each retelling. Despite reassurances from Governor Sam Houston, committees of "public safety" formed to censor the mail and watch for abolitionists. County patrols had been authorized earlier, but few were established. By late 1860 many towns organized patrols, including Gainesville.

As elsewhere in the South, the Texas Democratic Party became militant in its defense of slavery. Despite efforts to forge a consensus, however, voters in Cooke County consistently cast a higher percentage of their ballots against the Democrats than the rest of the state. Concern for frontier defense and a lack of direct involvement in slavery, led many county residents to reject the Democratic overtures. But the slave owner minority strongly endorsed the Democrats and embraced their push for secession after the election of Abraham Lincoln as president. John R. Diamond hosted a rally at his station on the Butterfield line in late November 1860. Most of those who attended owned slaves, and all but four signed a petition declaring that Lincoln's election made secession necessary and demanding that Houston call a convention. James J. Diamond, a Texas delegate to the 1860 Democratic convention, chaired the steering committee for the meeting at his brother's house, and he served on a similar committee for a caucus chaired by Bourland at Gainesville in December 1860. There Diamond and Bourland's push for disunion was opposed by William C. Young, who owned more slaves than anyone else in Cooke County. Ironically, Bourland had been lieutenant colonel of a regiment commanded by Young during the Mexican War, and they had fought together against Indians. Young was supported by district attorney William T. G. Weaver and chief justice Ralph G. Piper, but Diamond and Bourland prevailed, and a majority voted for a secession convention.

Although Governor Houston opposed secession, dates for the election of convention delegates appeared in newspapers. This strategy proved effective; three-fourths of Texas counties sent delegates, most of whom endorsed secession. James J. Diamond allegedly won in Cooke County, though the returns were "misplaced." Hoping the Texas legislature would not recognize the convention, Houston called a special session in January 1861. In spite of protests, the legislators approved the convention, which in turn passed a secession ordinance. James W. Throckmorton of North Texas opposed secession as a legislator and as a convention delegate, but only seven voted with him against disunion. When the convention called for a referendum on the secession ordinance, Throckmorton and William A. Ellet of Cooke County were among the eighteen legislators who presented a petition against secession at an Austin rally. In Cooke County, James J. Diamond and James G. Bourland stumped for disunion, but Abraham McNeese and John M. Crisp spoke against them. The election revealed a disturbing split for those who wanted to join the Confederacy: Texas returned a majority of more than three to one for secession, but Cooke County cast 61 percent of its votes against disunion.

As many feared, secession brought civil war. Seeking to allay concerns on the frontier, Confederate officials organized units for defense. Many in Cooke County joined a regiment led by Young. Three-fourths of his troopers opposed secession—including his lieutenant colonel, Throckmorton—but they joined to defend their homes from Indians. They occupied Federal posts in the Indian Territory, then began to depart for home after it became clear that the unit would be sent to battlefronts further east. When Young's men, despite his protests, became the 11th Texas Cavalry and crossed to the east bank of the Mississippi River, over two-thirds of them quit. Those who returned to Cooke County included Young; his son James D. Young; James J. Diamond, who had replaced Throckmorton; William C. Twitty; and Alexander Boutwell. Some who came home refused to serve again, joining a growing cohort suspected of disloyalty by Confederate officials. Others enlisted in local units, which had been organized to address the persistent concern for security throughout Texas. At Gainesville, the "Cooke County Home Guard Cavalry" mustered in June 1861. These were superseded by a statewide system of militia brigades. Bourland declined to command the Cooke County militia. Instead, upon his advice, the title of state brigadier general went to William R. Hudson, a fellow slaveholder from Cooke County. Hudson recruited about a thousand men into three battalions, one of which was commanded by Twitty.

Quite a few settlers had left after Texas seceded, but this did little to ease tensions. The refugees, who were denounced as abolitionists, were replaced by white and black newcomers from areas closer to the battlefronts. Conflict emerged as the struggling Confederate government adopted laws to draft men, collect taxes, impress goods, and sequester the property of enemies. Suspicions emerged that many joined the militia only to avoid conscription. Hudson originally worried that he could not find enough men, but recruiting became easier after the draft began. This led to another problem. As Hugh F. Young, commander of the militia in Grayson County and a former major in the 11th Texas Cavalry, complained, "Our families, our property, our all is now comparatively in the care and keeping of strangers." Rumors flew and "mutual distrust and dislike, criminations and recriminations" became common. Many turned again to proven local leaders and tactics, but now the violence focused on dissenters.

Vigilantism had actually persisted in North Texas since the war's beginning. Pryor of the *Dallas Herald* reported several lynchings in November 1861, adding, "We suppose they were all served about right." Cooke County commissioners appointed a new patrol—Boutwell, Hudson, slave owner James M. Peery, and deputy sheriff James B. Davenport Jr., who was the son of a slave owner—but they did little to stop vigilantism. Recalling that the murderers of a Gainesville barkeeper were lynched, a girl wrote, "Just why they were hanged, no one seemed to know or care." Cotton gin fires in early 1862 prompted Charles DeMorse, editor of the Clarksville *Standard*, to declare that many Unionists were "probably deserving of a hempen necklace." Downstate newspaper editors recalled the fires of 1860 and demanded action from Brigadier General Paul O. Hebert, commander of the Department of Texas. In response, Hebert in May 1862 imposed martial law, which would be administered by provost marshals.

Although they primarily served as enrolling officers, provost marshals could arrest any person they believed to be "injurious to the interests of the country." Their legal authority was analogous to that of a grand jury: if they found evidence of guilt, then they could order a prisoner to be tried by a military court. While such proceedings were to be conducted "as far as practical" in accordance with the rules for civil courts, "no unnecessary delays" for "strict and technical compliance" were allowed. After Hudson was appointed to command the Cooke county militia upon Bourland's recommendation, he selected the latter as provost marshal for his region. To assist in operations, Bourland not only had Hudson's militia but also Confederate units. These included new partisan ranger battalions such as the one led by John L. Randolph, among whose captains was James D. Young, formerly of the 11th Texas Cavalry.

Bourland came to believe that conscription had prompted the creation of a dangerous secret organization. Samuel McNutt, a carpenter from New York, wrote a protest against the draft, which was allegedly signed by more than thirty men and sent to the Confederate Congress. Newton J. Chance, a Kansas emigrant discharged from the Confederate army with disabilities, copied this list for Bourland, who exiled McNutt. Obediah B. Atkinson, a lieutenant in the Cooke County Home Guard Cavalry and Hudson's militia, took McNutt's place and enlisted perhaps two hundred men into a "Peace Party." Rumors circulated that this group communicated regularly with Unionists in Kansas who planned to invade Texas. Some settlers demanded that Bourland do something. His opportunity arose when one of Hudson's militia befriended Ephraim Chiles, who offered to initiate him into the Peace Party. Bourland asked the man to cooperate and learn more. The resulting report on Ephraim and his brother Henry intrigued a committee of inquiry organized and led by Bourland. The members included Hudson, Twitty, Peery, and James J. Diamond, as well as Charles L. Roff, a slave owner who commanded a company for Hudson. Bourland's committee next sent Chance to meet Henry Chiles. In an alarming report, Chance said that Chiles and his allies planned an uprising to support a Union invasion of Texas.

Bourland's committee decided to act. Hudson was absent, but his place was taken by Bourland's son-in-law, Samuel C. Doss; Twitty's father-in-law, Daniel Montague; and Peery's father, William. Bourland first sent a plea for help to Austin. Governor Francis R. Lubbock forwarded the request and those of others such as William C. Young to Hebert, but the general could not send troops. Instead, he temporarily accepted three companies of Hudson's militia into Confederate service, with James J. Diamond administering the oath of allegiance. Lubbock informed the

Gainesville leaders that they would have the full support of his administration for any actions they took. With this endorsement, Bourland acted. Twitty ordered a militia muster at daybreak on October 1, 1862. Many did not respond, and he ordered those in the ranks to surround the homes of all shirkers despite a driving rainstorm. The militia by noon had about seventy prisoners in a vacant store on the Gainesville square. A few escaped, including Atkinson, but some who tried to run or resist were shot. The prisoners were remarkably calm. Witnesses assumed that they expected to be rescued, but the large number of Twitty's militia, augmented by zealous volunteers, dissuaded at least two groups of Unionists, one of which was another company of Hudson's militia, from attacking. Tragically, fifteen of those who decided against a rescue were later arrested and hanged.

Frightened Confederate sympathizers in Gainesville welcomed reinforcements. The first was a Grayson County company of Hugh F. Young's militia led by Capt. John Russell, formerly of the 11th Texas Cavalry. Lubbock wrote to Col. Douglas H. Cooper, commanding the Indian Territory, asking him to send troops. In response, two partisan ranger companies arrived under captains Abner M. Marshall and John K. Bumpass. Capt. Nick Wilson led Company B of the 29th Texas Cavalry, whose colonel was DeMorse, into Gainesville on October 7. With this assistance, Bourland continued his arrests until he had about 150 prisoners.

A vigilante tribunal was quickly organized to try the prisoners in Gainesville. Chance and Boutwell held a rally on October 1, mustering support for Bourland before a town meeting at noon. William C. Young was elected to chair the town meeting. He chose five "good and true men" to select a dozen "good true and lawful men" to "investigate, examine, and decide upon all cases that should be brought before them." The five were James B. Davenport Jr., who had become sheriff; district clerk Aaron Hill, a Southern Methodist elder; William Peery; Chief Justice Ralph G. Piper; and slaveholder James B. Stone. After "careful and mature deliberation," the five chose jurors not for their "strong southern or secessionist predilections, or enmity toward Union men," but for "moderation, intelligence, and virtue." Their choices were endorsed in a referendum, giving the sanction of democracy to the "Citizens Court" that they had organized.

The twelve jurors chosen were Barrett, Doss, John W. Hamill, Hughes, James Jones, Reason Jones, Wiley Jones, J. Pope Long, Montague, Benjamin Scanland, William J. Simpson, and Thomas Wright. Among the seven who owned slaves, Montague and Wiley Jones were county commissioners and would be elected to the legislature. Another, Barrett, was a minister, while Hamill, a non-slaveholder, was a Southern Methodist minister who opposed abolitionism. They were all too old for the draft and none had been in the army, but Simpson was in Hugh F. Young's militia. Among the jurors, Barrett recalled, three were "very bitter against the accused," and others had suspicions. Their decision to convict on a majority vote was grim. Most of the prisoners never had slaves, which fostered suspicion that they were abolitionists, and most were eligible for the draft but did not enlist, thus they were shirkers.

Resolutions passed at the town meeting authorized the Citizens Court to convict and execute defendants. Piper swore in the court and those who testified. The prisoners could employ legal counsel, issue subpoenas, and cross-examine witnesses, but there is no evidence any of them did these things. Piper also served as a clerk for the court along with James M. Peery, and he worked with Hill, militia captain Cincinnatus Potter, and James E. Sheegog, a slaveholder and former county commissioner, to question witnesses and record their testimony. William W. Bourland, the provost marshal's son and a veteran of the 11th Texas Cavalry, acted as a constable. With Montague as foreman, the trials began on October 2. William C. Young served as prosecutor, and through his efforts the jurors acquitted most who came before them. Seven were condemned for Union sentiment and organizing the Peace Party: Henry and Ephraim Chiles, Henry S. Field, M. D. Harper, Leander W. P. "Jacob" Lock, William W. Morris, and Edward D. Hampton. All were hanged within seven days. Slave Bob Scott drove a wagon from under each after Boutwell put a rope around their necks, leaving them suspended from an elm on Pecan Creek. Two more, James T. Foster and Thomas B. Floyd, were shot as they tried to run.

The condemnation of seven men horrified Barrett. When he proposed surrendering the guilty prisoners to proper authorities, other jurors tried to have him expelled. He exploded after the sentencing of an eighth man to be hanged, denouncing his fellow jurors. Long rose to leave with him, but the others convinced them to stay by agreeing to convict only on a two-thirds vote. This change led to a reversal of the eighth man's conviction, and the jurors then worked quickly to acquit all of the other suspects to foil angry mobs, who twice tried to lynch the prisoners. By Saturday, October 11, the jury had reviewed all of the defendants without another condemnation. When someone reported that they had completed their deliberations, two men came into the courtroom and demanded twenty prisoners. Piper gave their list to one of the pair, who chose fourteen names. Believing the military would not protect any remaining prisoners, the jurors decided to wait until the next Saturday to free them.

The fourteen selected on October 11 were a diverse group, united primarily by their refusal to support the Confederacy. C. F. and George W. Anderson, Rama Dye, and William W. Wernell had been implicated during earlier trials. Three others had plotted to attack Gainesville on October 1: Benjamin C. Barnes, Henry Cockrum and James A. Powers, who may also have been singled out because he was Atkinson's brother-in-law. McNeese had opposed secession but was a captain in Hudson's militia. William R. Rhodes left a frontier defense company, perhaps deserting, while Samuel Carmichael had spoken against the Confederacy and refused to muster. Nathaniel M. Clark also opposed disunion, but the remainder—Thomas O. Baker, C. A. Jones, and Elliot M. Scott—did little to distinguish themselves. Boutwell hanged them in two groups, three on a chilly Sunday, October 12, and the rest on Monday, which proved to be little warmer.

The uneasy peace that settled over Cooke County after the adjournment of the Citizens Court was shattered by the murder of William C. Young on October 16. Young was ambushed as he led a posse along a tributary of the Red River in pursuit of unknown men who had killed a local hunter. The news inflamed emotions. When the jurors reassembled on October 18, several moderates were absent. Their places were taken by Chance, upon whom Montague bestowed the title of foreman, and slaveholder William W. Howeth, brother of the man who had shot James T. Foster. Montague and others who advocated retribution welcomed the newcomers. A third new juror, trooper James McPherson, was in fact a member of the Peace Party, which he must have hidden. Without Young's moderating influence, the Citizens Court retried and condemned nineteen prisoners who had been acquitted. Protests from Barrett and McPherson prompted Bourland to arrest the latter, but he was soon released.

The nineteen unfortunate men were hanged on October 19 under the supervision of James D. Young, the son of the slain colonel. Like the victims on October 12 and 13, many had been implicated in earlier testimony. Nine conspired to rescue their friends on the night of October 1: William B. Anderson, Barnibus Burch, Arphax R. Dawson, Hudson J. Esman, Curd Goss, William W. Johnson, David M. Leffel, John W. Morris and Gilbert Smith. Another, John M. Crisp, tried to bargain by offering information about others, but his proposals were rejected by the jurors. A similar appeal from Eli M. Thomas was spurned as well, while Alexander D. Scott stoically accepted his amended verdict. Richard N. Martin, a recruiter for the Peace Party, delivered an angry speech with the rope around his neck, denouncing his brother-in-law, William Boyles, for luring him into the group. Boyles was never caught by the Citizens

Court, but he was murdered in nearby Collinsville. The rest—Richard J. Anderson, John B. Miller, John A. Morris, M. W. Morris, William B. Taylor, and James A. Ward—were apparently condemned only for their membership in the Peace Party.

The poignant testimony of the condemned men illustrated the irony of the vigilante trials. Some in the Peace Party professed a strong commitment to the Union, but they were a minority in the organization, as were those who planned uprisings. The majority simply sought a method by which they could protect their families and homes on a violent frontier. Most had become convinced that the Confederacy could not survive, and they trusted the Peace Party to provide security by cooperative action until the Federals could restore order. Ironically, the concern for order and security among neighbors who supported the Confederacy led to an angry backlash that killed many innocent men. As for those who were fortunate enough to be acquitted and released, most of them fled, having learned a hard lesson about vigilantism and dissent on the Texas frontier.

Scott carried the bodies of the executed men to an empty building next to Bourland's headquarters on the town square. A few families claimed the remains of their relatives, some of them mutilated by hogs that pushed through a hole in the back wall, but most were left for the county to bury. Slaves were detailed to build rude coffins. Frank Foreman tore down an empty house for lumber, and then, when that was exhausted, wrapped the remainder in blankets and buried them in shallow graves along Pecan Creek. The next rain washed several bodies from the ground, while hogs uncovered others and fed upon them. A young girl saw a large hog drag her stepfather's arm through the streets of Gainesville.

The violence did not cease in Cooke County as Bourland demanded the arrest of Unionists elsewhere in North Texas. Testimony in the Citizens Court implicated some in Wise County. Names were sent to John W. Hale, commander of Hudson's militia at Decatur, and a sweep was made. A commission of two dozen, led by Southern Methodist minister James R. Bellamy, condemned five men: Ira Burdick, John M. Conn, Jim McKinn, Henry R. Maple, and another known only by his last name, Ward. Sheriff Robert G. Cates was their executioner, hanging the men from wagons on October 18. Several were arrested in Denton County, but all were set free. Some of those tried at Gainesville asserted that militia in Sherman had joined the Peace Party. Sixteen were tried by a commission of two dozen men in Sherman, but they were spared through the intervention of state district judge Robert W. Waddell and Throckmorton, who had resigned from the 6th Texas Cavalry and returned home to nearby Collin County. Throckmorton and Waddell convinced the mob to transfer their prisoners to the Confederate district court at Tyler. That court set their bail at a paltry $200. Most posted bond and scattered; only two returned on November 13 for a trial, and they were both acquitted. One of the two, Clement Wood, quietly went home. The other, Richard Lively, assailed his accusers in local newspapers and was killed after the war by pro-Confederate guerrillas.

The dismissal by the Confederate district court was seconded by Waddell in his state court. His chance to curb the violence in Cooke County came when Joel F. DeLemeron was brought before him on November 7, 1862. The grand jury that had indicted DeLemeron for helping refugees to flee from Cooke County included Citizens Court members Wiley Jones, James B. Stone, and Montague. The evidence was strong that DeLemeron had also proposed an attack on Gainesville. The trial jury convicted him in spite of Waddell's instructions that if they had a "reasonable doubt," then they had to acquit. DeLemeron was then spared when Waddell refused to sentence him to death. He was sent to the state prison, whence he was released after the war.

Barrett had argued that guilty prisoners should be turned over to military authorities, but he did not realize the grisly role that some of them played. On October 4, 1862, Randolph wrote to Bourland and William C. Young, asking if any of his men had been implicated by the Citizens Court. He added that it would be his "greatest pleasure to arrest them, and if necessary assist you in hanging them. " Days later, he marched into Sherman with over two dozen prisoners from his battalion, all of them accused of being Unionists. He directed a court martial that condemned three of the company led by James D. Young, who hanged them at his father's home. Randolph himself conducted a "wholesale hanging" from which "no man who was proved to belong to the [Peace Party] was spared." Alarmed, many of his troops "began to desert and scatter like wild buffaloes." Like the vigilante tribunals, the court martial ran its course, and Randolph sent a handful of men to the Confederate district court.

James D. Young did not stop with the execution of three men from his company. He tracked Daniel Welch, a deserter who allegedly killed William C. Young, to the Indian Territory, took him to the Young homestead, and hanged him in front of his late father's slaves. He then burned the body on the site where the colonel had been killed. His next victim was E. Junius Foster, an editor in Sherman who had published several editorials on the vigilante violence, including one applauding the murder of William C. Young. Three horsemen—Young, Chance, and an accomplice—confronted Foster as he was closing his office. Young demanded that Foster recant his statement about his father. When he refused, a rider put a double-barreled shotgun in his side and pulled both triggers. Young continued until his military superiors demanded that he resign. He quit the Confederate army after penning one last diatribe against Unionists.

The zeal of Confederate authorities to punish those in the Peace Party extended far beyond Texas. Frederick W. Sumner, a Unionist from Sherman, fled but was imprisoned in Little Rock. He was joined in his cell by Atkinson and John Davidson, who had also escaped and joined Company I of the Confederate 6th Missouri Cavalry, led by John T. Crisp, the uncle of John M. Crisp, who was hanged in Gainesville. John T. Crisp had enrolled a company in Cooke County with the promise that they would be Missouri home guards, but they were drafted by the Confederate army. Atkinson and Davidson had provided sketchy details of the hangings to their new comrades, and several got letters telling them of the death of relatives or friends. When some deserted, the duo, as well as Crisp, were arrested. Rumors of mutiny led to Crisp's release, but the Cooke County pair waited with Sumner until the Federals occupied Little Rock during the fall of 1863. Allegations also surfaced about Brigadier General Albert Pike's involvement in the Peace Party, but he fended off such dangerous accusations.

News of the Great Hanging spread throughout the Confederacy. DeMorse of the Clarksville *Standard* and Robert W. Loughery of the Marshall *Texas Republican* printed a letter from Throckmorton, who dismissed the victims as "refugees and suspected persons." Other Texas editors proved ready to believe in a Union conspiracy. Edward H. Cushing of the Houston *Telegraph* wrote his account from official reports and condoned the lynchings. Willard Richardson of the Galveston *News*, I. R. Worrall of the Austin *Texas State Gazette*, and David Richardson of the *Texas Almanac Extra* printed eyewitness accounts and added their approval. Ironically, the San Antonio *Herald*, which had opposed secession, published the most vitriolic support of the hangings. Because Houston was the principal clearinghouse for Texas news, Willard Richardson's opinions reappeared in most major Confederate newspapers. Most agreed with the Little Rock *True Democrat* that "By the fortunate discovery of this scheme Texas has been enabled to purge herself of traitors."

Confronted with the Great Hanging, the Jefferson Davis administration largely ignored the affair, while Texas officials condoned it. Davis had already removed Hebert on October 10 for his imposition of martial law. The Great Hanging belied Hebert's argument that prisoners were "tried with all the facilities of defense as in the ordinary common law trial," but nothing more was done. Governor Lubbock at first was appalled by the reports, but William C. Young's murder ended his reservations. Adjutant General J. Y. Dashiell wrote to Hudson that while the hangings were "deplorable," the "strictest measures of the sternest justice "had to be imposed on any "Traitors that pollute the soil of our state." When Lubbock called a special session of the legislature in February 1863, he endorsed Hudson's actions. Hale represented Cooke County, and he joined a majority of his fellow legislators in approving Hudson's reimbursement. Davis did not protest, and Lubbock became his advisor on the Trans-Mississippi later in 1863.

Dissent in North Texas did not end with the Great Hanging, and Bourland was entrusted with its suppression. Twitty's companies patrolled under the command of John R. Baylor until January 1863. Three months later, they formed the nucleus of a Frontier Battalion mustered into regular service by Bourland. Twitty was their first commander, but Smith P. Bankhead, who had been nominated for a brigadier generalship after his campaign against Germans in Central Texas, made changes when he took charge of the new Northern Subdistrict of Texas. The battalion expanded to six companies and Twitty and other participants in the Great Hanging—including Roff, James J. Diamond, and Samuel P. C. Patton—became subordinates of Bourland. Renewed violence led Bankhead to ask for a transfer from "this Godforsaken country." His replacement, Henry E. McCulloch, a brigadier general with a similar reputation for battling dissent in Central Texas, offered amnesty to those who would enlist, but he added threats of violence for those who did not. He promoted Bourland to lieutenant colonel and then colonel, and gave him control over all Confederate units west of Grayson County. McCulloch believed North Texas needed an "energetic, fighting, hanging man" to combat dissent, and he retained Bourland in command through the war's end despite many protests from Confederate and state officers in the region.

The end of the war encouraged dissenters in North Texas to believe that redress would finally come. Federals finally landed at Galveston on June 19, 1865, but diplomatic concerns dictated that most were sent to the Rio Grande. None could be spared initially for remote regions such as North Texas, where Bourland ironically was selected by Federal officials to manage the parole of local Confederates. Andrew J. Hamilton, a prominent Unionist who had fled Texas, returned as provisional governor in August 1865 and delivered angry speeches promising justice, but he made crucial mistakes in his selection of state leaders. For North Texas, he relied upon Throckmorton, unaware that he believed order and security should be trusted to men who had supported the Confederacy. Among the new appointments was William T. G. Weaver, who became a Confederate officer after opposing secession, as judge for the district that included Cooke County.

Hamilton's appointments and the lack of a strong Federal presence impeded efforts to prosecute those responsible for the Great Hanging. Bourland, James D. Young, and the jurors of the Citizens Court were indicted on November 11, 1865. Allegedly Weaver deliberately issued "faulty" writs; he denied this, but they were not served until a week after he adjourned, allowing many of the guilty to escape. Thirty-seven residents of Cooke County, including Atkinson and Davidson, who had survived the prison in Little Rock, petitioned Hamilton to remove several officials. He did so on November 10, but not in time to prevent a debacle. The petitioners also asked for Federal troops. When ex-Confederates added demands for security from Indians and outlaws, Hamilton contacted Major General George A. Custer, who sent two companies. These men arrested several who had evaded Weaver, but county officials allowed many to escape again. When more troops were sent, they were instructed not to become involved "in matters of crimes committed before the occupation of the state by Federal troops," a clear signal that the national government would take no action against those responsible for the Great Hanging.

Vengeance for wartime atrocities became the topic of angry debates during the state constitutional convention in February 1866. The assembly was dominated by ex-Confederates; prominent among the delegates were Throckmorton and Bumpass, who commanded a company at Gainesville in October 1862. Also present from Cooke County was James M. Lindsay, whom the Quitman *Clipper* claimed had participated in the Great Hanging. Throckmorton led the push for conciliation, asking the delegates to "bury, upon the altar of our common country, all the recent past." Those who opposed him were pleased when the wartime debt, much of which they believed had been spent for the persecution of dissenters, was repudiated. They failed, however, to block the adoption of Ordinance Number 11, which barred the prosecution of anyone for acts performed under Confederate authority. A furious minority recalled the Great Hanging and condemned Hudson as a "fiend in human shape," while Hamilton denounced the measure for "legislating wholesale robbery and murder throughout the land."

Throckmorton defeated Elisha M. Pease, a former governor and noted Unionist, for the governor's seat, while conservatives dominated the legislature, effectively closing the door on state justice for victims of the Great Hanging. Weaver presided over the acquittals of six jurors from the Citizens Court: Doss, Reason and Wiley Jones, Scanland, Simpson, and Wright. Some claimed that bribes were paid, but Ordinance Number 11 blocked any effective prosecution, and it was unlikely that a jury to convict them could be mustered from among the remaining residents who had supported the Confederacy. But the story of the Great Hanging refused to fade entirely. Custer testified to Congress about the affair, and Federal officials heard that Throckmorton had encouraged rather than blocked vigilantes. Throckmorton wrote to James J. Diamond, who had become the editor of the Houston *Dispatch,* and asked him to publish a denial, but the damage was done. When a Republican majority in Congress imposed military reconstruction in 1867, Throckmorton and many other officials were removed for a variety of offenses.

The Republican ascendancy renewed hope for justice in North Texas. One of the new appointees was Atkinson, while Chief Justice John E. Wheeler, who was arrested but freed during the Great Hanging, was allowed to stay in office. Weaver was replaced with Hardin Hart by Pease, Throckmorton's successor as governor, in December 1867. Hart, a Unionist whose brother Martin had been hanged by Confederates, mounted a final attack on those who had participated in the Great Hanging. Barrett and Long, each of whom had fled the state but returned, were tried by Hart in December 1868. Defended by Throckmorton and Weaver, both men were acquitted by a Cooke County jury. Hart also tried Bourland, who actually had an executive pardon from President Andrew Johnson under his 1865 amnesty proclamation, but the result was the same.

Among the witnesses at Bourland's trial in December 1868 was James Jones, who moved to the Indian Territory in 1865 after threatening to shoot Boutwell. In return for his testimony against Bourland, Jones was given immunity for his role in the Great Hanging and for a murder indictment against him in November 1863 for an unrelated incident. Jones also testified against James D. Young, who remained at large until 1871, after Hart had been succeeded by another Unionist, Christopher C. Binkley. On December 20, a jury acquitted Young for the murder of Foster. When his wartime accomplice, Chance, was finally arraigned in 1885, Young confessed in court that he killed Foster. Because Young had been acquitted earlier, both men went free.

Chance's acquittal ended the trials of those involved in the Great Hanging. Nine jurors from the Citizens Court—Barrett, Chance, Doss, Reason Jones, Wiley Jones, Long, Scanland, Simpson, and Wright—had been acquitted by a legal jury. Hughes, like Bourland, had gotten a presidential pardon, but unlike the latter he was never tried and all charges were dropped. James Jones earned immunity, but no records remain of dispositions for Hamill, Howeth, McPherson, and Montague. Howeth stayed in Gainesville, but Hamill and McPherson may have followed Montague into exile. The latter was in Mexico until 1876, when he returned to his daughter's Cooke County home, where she lived with her husband, Twitty, and died within a few months.

Montague need not have stayed away so long. No Cooke County jury would convict him because most of them had supported efforts to protect order and security from Indians, outlaws and abolitionists before the Civil War and dissenters during the war. They would not betray their leaders. To do so was to risk not only legal retribution but the personal turmoil of admitting that they had been wrong. Confronted with an uncomfortable choice, they chose to endorse what was done and not ask questions whose answers could be quite disturbing. The desire of people for order and security not only led to the tragedy of the Great Hanging, but successfully thwarted justice. In years to come, most would focus on trying to forget until the Texas State Historical Association published two primary accounts of the affair, providing modern historians with the opportunity to replace inaccurate popular memories with a more truthful, and useful, history.

THE GREAT HANGING AT GAINESVILLE

A REPRINT BY

THE TEXAS STATE HISTORICAL ASSOCIATION

Printed in the United States of America

Austin, 1961

The Texas State Historical Association

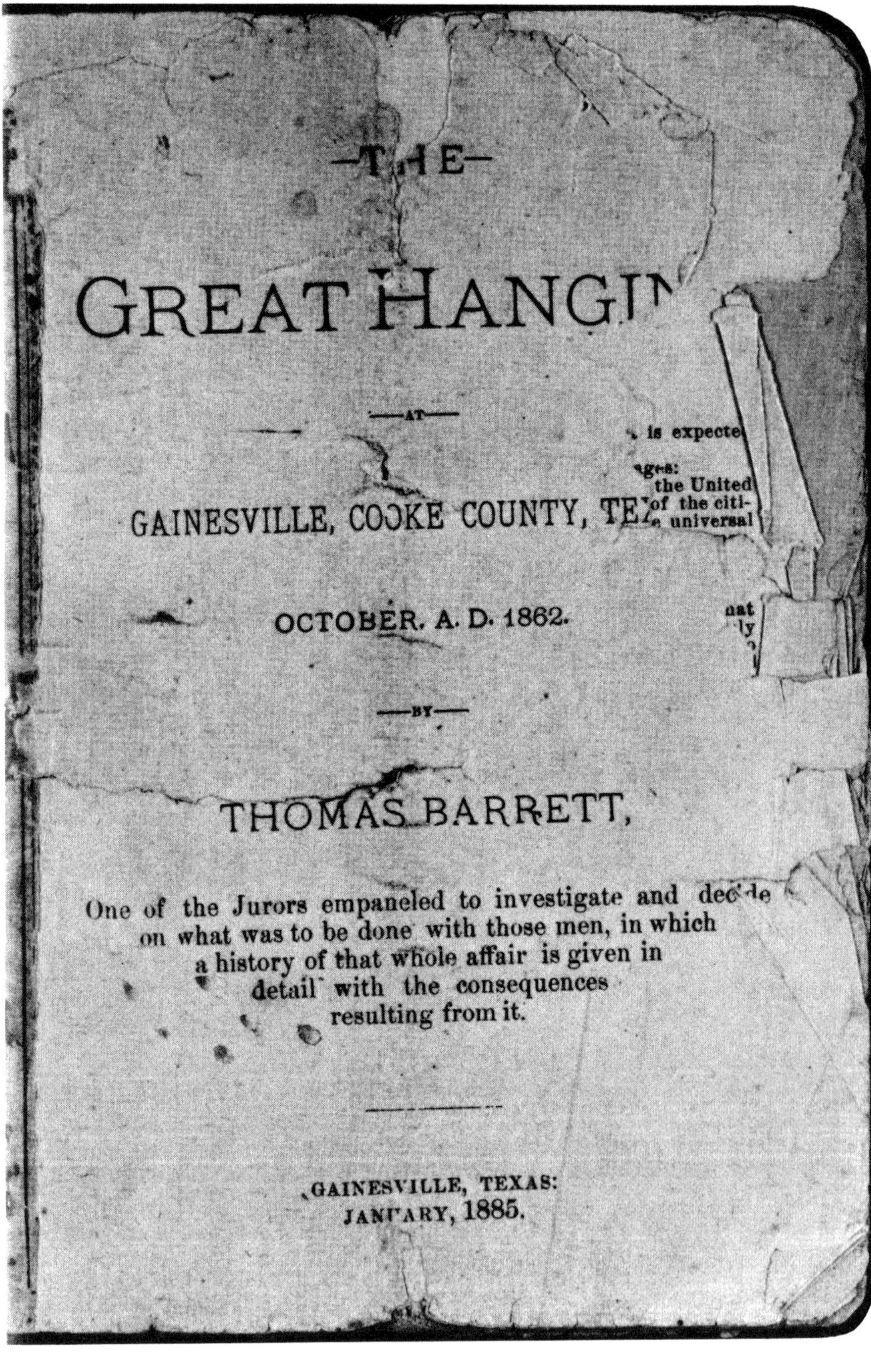

THE

GREAT HANGI

AT

GAINESVILLE, COOKE COUNTY, TE

OCTOBER. A. D. 1862.

BY

THOMAS BARRETT,

One of the Jurors empaneled to investigate and decide on what was to be done with those men, in which a history of that whole affair is given in detail with the consequences resulting from it.

GAINESVILLE, TEXAS:
JANUARY, 1885.

Title page of the Vandale copy of *The Great Hanging*

PREFACE

As early as January, 1861, a unionist plan to dismember Texas was proposed in the Southern Intelligencer. This plan initially was to be operative in Cooke, Wise, Grayson, Collin, Denton, and other counties of North Texas if the state attempted to secede from the Union. There were no immediate results, but beginning in September, 1861, a secret "Peace Party" was organized in the North Texas area. The Great Hanging pamphlet is a participant's account of events in the fall of 1862, which verged on a reign of terror following the discovery by Confederate officials in Texas of the unionist sympathizers, their activities, and plans.

Traditionally the annual meeting program of the Texas State Historical Association contains a documentary item of particular historical interest in the Texana field. Thomas Barrett's Great Hanging at Gainesville was first reproduced as a part of the printed program for 1961. This account was suggested by Cooper K. Ragan, a member of the Publications Committee, an advanced collector on the Civil War, and a leading light in the Houston Civil War Round-Table program. Seymour V. Connor, Roger Conger, Walter Long, and Herbert Gambrell added strong insistence. This is the first separate reprinting of this remarkable account.

The offering, on this centenary of the beginning of the War for Southern Independence, is unquestionably timely. This publication and that of the program were made possible in a quite real way through the cooperation of that independent and constructive-thinking entrepreneur of The Steck Company, R. H. Porter.

The Great Hanging at Gainesville pamphlet, which is here reproduced, is one of the choicest titles of Texana and, perhaps, one of the rarest. Earl Vandale, the great Khan of Texana, probably suffered more in acquiring this item than with any other single one. Vandale ran advertisements for years in the North Texas newspapers and actually made lots of house-to-house calls in the countryside about Gainesville seeking a copy of this work. His persistency was finally rewarded when he located and purchased in the countryside east of Gainesville the copy here reproduced.

When Vandale finally acquired the Great Hanging pamphlet, he did one of the things he was much wont to do. He dispatched a telegram. This one was to Herbert Fletcher, bookseller and Texana-finder de luxe at Houston. The telegram read, "Have Great Hanging. Come see it." Naturally Fletcher had been seeking the item for Vandale throughout many years. The telegram was all that Fletcher needed. He got together hurriedly Matt Weeks, Dr. Henry Maresh, and Louis Lenz. The party set out by automobile immediately for Amarillo. Upon arrival in Amarillo the occasion called for a party in honor of the Great Hanging which was given by Bishop Laurence J. FitzSimon at the Amarillo Country Club. Following the party, Herbert Fletcher sat up the rest of the night reading the Great Hanging, after which he and his group returned immediately to Houston.

The University of Texas acquired its first copy of the pamphlet in the Earl Vandale Collection of Texana. Within the past several months another copy has been acquired by the University from the Frank Caldwell Collection of Texana. Frank Caldwell also suffered mightily in acquiring, after searching for more than twenty years, one copy of the Great Hanging. Caldwell traded for his copy a brace of the finest pistols he ever owned. Sometime after 1936 the Library of Congress acquired a copy. These three represent all the known copies extant.

The printer who set the type for the original of The Great Hanging *in 1885 apparently ran short of periods and also of some letters, for spaces exist in a few words and at the end of some sentences. These omissions have been corrected for the sake of clarity. They are the only editorial changes in the reprint.*

The pamphlet is much in the folklore of Gainesville, Cooke County, and surrounding North Texas. Mostly the stories tell that in the post Civil War times it was unsafe to possess a copy. When the venerable C. N. Jones was approaching octogenarian standing, he told me that although he had been interested in Gainesville history through a long life, it had been only a few years before blindness overtook him that a lifetime friend took him to an attic, uncovered a Great Hanging pamphlet, and let him read it.

Although the pamphlet was "bad medicine" for years it is a valuable document of local history and of the Civil War. It tells its own behind-the-lines story and is probably as challenging in 1961 as the day it was published.

H. Bailey Carroll

Austin
October 1, 1961

–THE–

GREAT HANGING

–AT–

GAINESVILLE, COOKE COUNTY, TEXAS

OCTOBER, A.D. 1862

–BY–

THOMAS BARRETT,

One of the Jurors empaneled to investigate and decide
on what was to be done with those men, in which
a history of that whole affair is given in
detail with the consequences
resulting from it.

GAINESVILLE, TEXAS:
JANUARY, 1885.

Introduction.

When a writer endeavors to write a history of any event, it is expected that he will give his reasons for so doing.

I shall give some of the reasons for writing the following pages:

In the first place, there is not one person in every thousand in the United States who understand this thing, and I will add that very few of the citizens of Gainesville and Texas understand much about it. The universal idea (almost) is that these men were hung because they were union men, which is not the fact, which the following pages will abundantly show. Do not be startled, reader, at this statement, for facts are stubborn things and never yield to opinions formed from uncertain rumor.

It being thought by many, very many, persons whose heads are level that the world should know the whole truth of this affair; and I being the only man who could give it in detail, I have been strongly urged for years to write this history. For reasons satisfactory to myself, I have refused till now. But I consider the time has come when it is not only prudent but necessary that a history in detail of this whole thing should be published to the world. And inasmuch as I was on that jury and a public man, being a doctor and a preacher, madam rumor with her thousand false tongues has represented me as being the very ringleader in that affair, when I was opposed to all that hanging from the beginning to the end. And here I would notify the reader that I shall often refer to the course I pursued in opposition to violence, for the reason that I did nearly all the speaking in opposition to violent measures.

There are several important circumstances which took place which cannot be fairly stated without telling what I said and did. This is my apology for telling my own course. No individual need be uneasy for fear his name should come out in an unfavorable way. I shall state circumstances and avoid calling names, that my history may leave every man where he is now.

To the people of the United States, this history is respectfully dedicated by the Author.

Gainesville, Texas, January 5th, 1885.

THE GREAT HANGING

—AT—

Gainesville, Cooke Co., Texas

CHAPTER I

The Great Hanging at Gainesville, Cooke County, October, A. D. 1862.

I want every reader of the following pages to read the introduction first as that will give him a fair introduction to the subject.

The war between the states, north and south, having existed more than a year; the war fever having risen to boiling heat; the Confederate congress passed the conscript-law. This law was very offensive to many and particularly to those who were afterwards members of the organization for which they where hung. In riding through the country I called at a steam mill and found about a dozen men; the mill was not running, so we had a good chance to talk. Some one named the conscript-law; its effect was like a spark lighting on powder; all was in a blaze of opposition as deep and as fierce as it was possible for it to exist in the human mind was plainly manifested.

After much talk and hard things being said, one man, who seemed to be a leader, boldly declared he was ready to head a company to resist the conscript-law. Up to this time I had said but little, but now I thought it was my time as I had their confidence and was the family physician of some of them. I called his attention to the fact that in the event that he attempted to carry out his plans, he could not expect anything but an awful failure and that he and all those who were in arms would be killed, and after saying all I could to dissuade him from taking that course, I left him, but he abandoned the idea and made a speech to a crowd, confessing that he had proposed to head a company to resist the conscript-law, but he said he abandoned the idea.

This man afterward went overboard. This was no doubt the entering wedge to the organization which is yet to be named.

For some time after, there was strong and mysterious things said which were not understood by the great mass of people. I heard them and others heard them; we could form no idea what could be up. We could hear war news frequently before it got into our newspapers. There was so much of this going on that I became convinced that there was some kind of organization in the country, and others came to to the same conclusion. We afterwards learned that the members of the organization yet to be named had regular mails to and from Kansas jayhawkers, which will be stated in full in its proper place.

At this period Texas had been laid off in military districts, and all the officers appointed to completely organize the militia. And now I come to the point in my history to give an account of the organization alluded to above.

The mail-carrier, who carried the mail from Gainesville south, was staying all night at a hotel in Gainesville, and a man who was a member of the organization was there also. This man was considerably under the influence of liquor. This man told the mail-carrier enough about this organization to excite his curiosity and his suspicion, so he asked a number of questions about it; the intoxicated man told him to go to a certain man and that man would initiate him and tell him all about it. The mail-carrier said nothing about what he had heard, but started south with the mail next morning. By the time he got into Denton county he had thought so much of the strange mysterious affair, that he came to the settled conclusion that there was something very dangerous to the community on hand, and the people unapprised and unprepared for it.

That it might come upon them at the midnight hour, with all the horrors of a savage massacre, and he was not far wrong as the sequel will prove by the confessions of the members of the organization which I am approaching in my history.

This mail-carrier came to the conclusion that he would inform the military authority of what he had heard at Gainesville, and did so, through a military officer, who gave information to the military at Gainesville, as that was headquarters of this division of the military.

When this mail-carrier came back to Gainesville, the military questioned him and after learning all they could from him, he was sent to be initiated. He went and took the oath of secrecy and took what will be known in this history as the first degree, though the members of this organization did not so call it. After taking this first degree he was told if he would take another oath he would be informed of the whole thing. But he refused to go any further, and when he reported to the military, there being nothing in this first degree to make a fuss about, the anxiety was great to know what was in what I shall call the second degree.

The military selected a man who had been connected with the Confederate army to go and be carried clear through if the road was one-hundred miles through, and a better man for this business would be hard to find.

This man went to this initiator and wormed himself into his favor, about in this way (I heard him tell it more than once). He spoke of having been connected with the Confederate army in a manner which was well calculated to convey the idea that he was not sound in the faith.

This caused the initiator to ask him how he was pleased with the condition of things. The man seeking to be initiated answered, not very well, and remarked if you had been where I have been and seen and heard what I have, you would not be pleased yourself. This was a precious morsel for the initiator; he bent forward with a smile and was in this way thrown completely off of his guard. And the organization, about which I am writing was named, and the man wishing to be initiated, not only nibbled at it, but he bit heavy, swallowing the hook bait and all. So he took both degrees, saying it was the very thing for the times.

The man that was initiated asked the initiator to give him the names of some of the members that he might know who to approach, and he got quite a number of names. This man then asked the initiator to initiate another man, but he objected; saying that the man was a strong southern man. He was, said the other, but I have worked on him and he is all right now. So the agreement was that the other man was to be initiated next day. They met next day and the man was put through. The two men questioned the initiator till they found out much of the intentions of the members of the organization, but not all, for those leaders generally kept some of the most objectionable things back till they proved a man. But these men found out enough to know that if this thing was carried out it would devastate and ruin the country.

Don't be surprised at the strength of the language at the conclusion of the above

THOMAS BARRETT

From A. Morton Smith, *The First 100 Years in Cooke County*, San Antonio (The Naylor Company), 1955.

sentence, for the truth must come, and when you hear, you will say the language is not stronger than the case demands.

The next thing to be done, was, for these men to report to the military at Gainesville. The men lived near each other, but in going to report at Gainesville they went different routes. This was done to guard against suspicion. I tell you they were old ones.

When they met in Gainesville, they went to the headquarters of the military, where counsellors met. I do not know how many composed that counsel, but they formed their plans well.

CHAPTER II

After the men spoken of in the previous chapter had finished their report, the military sent out orders for all the militia of Cooke county to report at Gainesville, armed and equipped for service at the earliest practical hour next day. Those over age were pressed into the service. I was exempt in three cases, and a special order was dispatched to me in the night to be in Gainesville early next morning. One company was ordered from Wise, Denton and Grayson counties each; one company was asked for and sent from Fort Washita.

The night before these soldiers were to report in the morning, squads of men were sent out in different parts of the county, and directed to watch and not let the men whose names they had, leave in the night, and as soon as it was light enough in the morning, to close in and arrest the men. In this way, it was said, twenty were arrested the first grab. The arresting continued for about thirteen days and nights. How many were arrested, I have no means of knowing, having kept no account at the time, but I suppose there was not less than one hundred and fifty, and perhaps more.

There was a good many arrested who had connection with the organization.

There were squads of men in every part of the country, and they arrested every man that they suspicioned, and in this way a good many innocent men were arrested.

I must tell of one case: One of the squads came up with a man at his home, that they did not suspicion. They told him he must go with them and help arrest those men. He very readily agreed to do so, for it was dangerous to refuse in this high state of excitement; for I never saw such a state of excitement before, nor since, and hope never to see its equal again. But the man fell in with them, but he had no gun, and all the men except the prisoners had guns. When the squads arrived at the prison, and put them in, this man failed to go in, and some of the men knowing he had been with them and seeing he had no gun, ordered him in, and being a green case, he went in, and stayed in one or two days if I recollect right. I had been acquainted with him in Titus county, so he sent me word in reference to his case. I had him brought before the jury and being no evidence against him he was set at liberty.

But I must return from this digression.

Although I was notified to report early in the morning at Gainesville, being exempt from military duty and having an urgent professional call before morning, I visited a patient that morning before going to town. My patient was in a neighborhood where there had been several men arrested, and I began to learn something of the matter, and dispatched my business as speedily as possible, and I got to Gainesville about eleven o'clock.

When I arrived near town, there were crowds in sight in every direction, armed, pressing forward prisoners under guard. The deepest and most intense excitement that I ever saw prevailed. Reason had left its throne. The mind of almost every man I saw seemd to be unhinged, and wild excitement reigned supreme. When I arrived on the square, there were perhaps three or four hundred armed men in town and in sight.

These with the unarmed, constituted a crowd whose words and actions seemed to indicate an upheaving of the most dangerous character, because it was known that the members of that clan were sworn to go to the assistance of any member who was arrested. Aside the sequel will show that nothing but the overpowering numbers in arms prevented desperate fighting the next night.

The supposition at that time was, that the clan was strong enough to make a desperate fight.

Soon after I arrived on the square I heard hanging spoken of. I found the tree had been selected, that same old historic elm, with its long and bending limbs, which was afterwards used for that purpose.

The crowd seemed to be settling down on beginning to hang.

I opposed it with all the power within me. Others also opposed it, and about the time we were in the heat of contention, the church bell rang for a meeting of the crowd for consultation. The ringing of this bell put an end to all plans, in order to see what would be the result of that meeting. This was a military move, sanctioned by soldiers and citizens.

The meeting was called to order and a chairman appointed. A motion was made and carried for the chair to appoint five men to select a jury to decide upon the course to be pursued with these men. This committee selected twelve men, and my name was reported as one of them. My first thought was, not to serve as one of them, when I took the situation under consideration; I at once saw that unless there was considerable influence in that jury against extreme violence, there was great danger of awful work, so I consented to serve, intending to oppose all extreme violence, which I did. And here I will state the excitement was so great that every man found it necessary to exercise much caution in reference to what he said or did. This condition of things had its influence with me in deciding this question.

The jury was instructed to go into a fair examination and bring accused and witnesses face to face and decide, and they would abide by their decision.

The meeting adjourned, and the jury met and organized, and night came on. The militia and others had been coming in all day, and after dark they continued to come.

Squads of men were sent to different parts of the county to ascertain what was going on, for an attack was expected, which would cause desperate fighting. A double line of sentinels were put around the town.

One squad that was out came up with a company of men who belonged to this clan, supposed to be about seventy. The lieutenant of the squad knew the captain of the company composing the men of the organization about which I am writing, and made an attempt to talk to him. The captain objected and ordered him to hush but the lieutenant insisted on having a talk. The captain again ordered him to hush, and ordered his men to be ready, and when the lieutenant heard the ticking of the triggers of the guns, and knowing that he was not able with his little squad to contend against so many, he took his squad off in the brush and directed them to keep out of danger, and watch as well as they could; and having seen the company file off in the direction of Gainesville, he concluded they were going there to make an attack. The lieutenant, as a good spy, set out to beat the company to town. He run his horse so hard and in such haste that he found it necessary to stop on the way and get a fresh horse.

He arrived at Gainesville, gave the alarm, and immediately the men were paraded and placed in order of battle on the streets with orders to lie on their arms all night.

About fifteen or twenty men had gone about half a mile from the square to stay all night; I was one of the men. We were ordered to the square. When we got there I walked around and to see how the thing was going on. The soldiers were in line of battle and some in the houses making cartridges, others moving to and fro as is always the case in times of great excitement, everyone expecting a desperate fight before morning, for the clan was supposed to be stronger than they were. In reference to their strength, I may as well state what I learned from a man whom I sent word to to leave the country and stay away till the war ended, which he did. He told me when we met after the war closed that the organization was about seventeen hundred strong, including Cooke, Wise, Denton, Grayson and Collin counties.

But I must return to the thread of my narrative.

After seeing how everything was going on, and not having a gun and not having any desire to be in the fight, I went into a friend's house and asked the lady for a pillow and turning a chair down on the carpet slept till morning. There was no attack, consequently no fighting.

Here I must record what was going on in another part of the county as we learned in the jury-room from a man who was one of the clan. This man stated that he came to Gainesville the day that the first arrests were made; not having been arreste, stayed till evening, and learned all he could, and knowing that the clan were to meet at a certain place in the cross-timbers, he wanted to carry news to them. He applied for a pass to leave town, but was refused, and he having turned his horse in a pasture, he worked his way to the pasture, got his horse and went to the meeting. He said he found twenty-seven men armed and equipped; having appointed their captain and sent a courier to the company which has been named. He also stated that they were noisy to be led on to the assistance of their friends. He said he told them that he had been there most of the day and had come to inform them that it would be madness to go to attack the armed men in Gainesville, as there was such an overwhelming force there, that they would be marching to certain death. He said when he told them the condition at town, some said they would go and surrender; others said they would bushwhack, but they finally appointed a meeting the next night, but we learned that only three attended the meeting.

It can be plainly seen from what has been stated, that nothing but the overpowering numbers at Gainesville prevented one of those bloody massacres which sometimes take place in war.

But the second morning came and no attack was made, but the intense excitement was almost universal.

There was some talk of taking the prisoners out and hanging or shooting all of them, but it was not done.

I have no language adequate to convey to the mind of the reader a full idea of the deep and dangerous condition of the excitement up to this time. Those opposed to extreme punishment found it necessary to be extremely cautious if they made a remark in favor of mercy.

While the multitude did not at this time know the full intention of the clan, enough was known to give the idea that if the clan carried out its designs, the country would be thrown into a bloody war, with neighbor against neighbor, and in some cases the brother against brother, and in some cases the father against the son and the son against the father, and a man's foes would be of his own household.

The second day dawned and no attack being made, the jury met.

And now comes the tug of war. I would here remind the reader of what I have said in the introduction; I shall not call names and tell what they said and did. I shall tell what was done so as to leave every man as near as possible where he stands now.

I shall tell the course I pursued, inasmuch as my course has been misrepresented far and near, as far as I am known. I being a public man, a doctor and a preacher, some will object to the course I am pursuing in regard to myself. Let them object, I have weighed the consequences and am prepared to meet them.

I shall tell more of this in reference to this as I proceed in this history.

The jury met and passed an order that a majority should rule. I opposed this, and wanted it unanimous, or at any rate, two-thirds, but the majority rule was adopted. As far as could be done the leaders were tried first.

Right here, before proceeding further, it is important to give a detailed account of the course pursued in influencing individuals to become members of the organization, also signs, pass-words, grips and oaths. They would approach a man, talk some about the war and remark that there was something up. And when asked what it was, the answer was a peace party and a party to keep down jayhawking and to protect the families of those men who were in the war, and if their property was taken from them to make those who took it give it up, and bring about peace, and protect the soldiers when they came home from the army, even if they desired to pursuade them to go back and do better.

They told them that if they would take the oath of secrecy they would give the sign, pass-word and grip.

If the individuals agreed to take the oath, after taking it they were told when they met up with a man, the situation admitted, to pass the fingers of the right hand slowly over the right ear; the answer to this was for the man to pass the finger of the left hand slowly over the left ear, but to guard against all mistakes when they approached a man and gave him the sign and he seemed to answer it, to be sure he understood and answered the sign, he was to be asked: where he got his horse or any article about him. If he said in Arizona, he was all right and could be approached.

The grip to distinguish in a crowd or in the dark this: consisted in the common shake of the hand with the end of the forefinger pressing tolerably hard on the inside of the wrist.

They sometimes gave this sign, pass-word and grip to their friends, telling them that if there was any uprising to give them and they would save themselves and property. Telling nothing more.

They also stated that this organization existed in both northern and southern armies, and if they became sufficiently numerous they would stop the fighting and restore the constitution and union.

Here it is proper to state all of this was not told to all of the men, but all of this came up in the various confessions.

This constituted what I shall call the first degree, though they did not so call it. When they got through with this first degree, they would tell the man that if he would take another oath, they would tell him all they intended to do, if he consented. They swore him to secrecy and to do all he could for the north and to do all he could against the south, to reinstate the constitution and go to the relief of any member who should be arrested, and if a member betrayed them and their plans, they were to kill him if they had to follow him to the end of the earth, and no death was too bad for him to die. If he did not flinch, they then told the plan. They told the favored few all their plans, but to the great mass they only told part of their plans; all being sworn to obey their leaders.

The confederate government had a large amount of ammunition at Sherman which was guarded day and night. Cooke county had about four hundred pounds of powder and other ammunition to suit it.

Their plans were to rise in the night, take all the ammunition at Sherman and Gainesville and throw the country without ammunition and take the country and hold its property and all, and no man's person or property was to be respected, unless he had their sign, pass-word and grip. This and other things will appear when I come to speak particularly of the confessions.

Their Confessions

There were a few who seemed to know nothing but what was in the first degree. But an overwhelming majority confessed that they knew of this uprising in the night and taking the ammunition, as before stated. The most confessed that they had a monthly mail to the Kansas Jayhawkers and these Kansas Jayhawkers had promised to come to their assistance as soon as it rained there, having been a long dry spell. They said one of their clan was at that time in a two horse wagon to carry and bring the monthly mail, giving out that he was going to St. Louis on business. This man was arrested on his way home. They said some of the men who guarded the ammunition at Sherman belonged to their clan, and they had been down there and got a supply of ammunition. Here I will state that these men had more ammunition and guns in better order than any men in the county, and some of them slept with their guns under their pillows.

But to return. These men, when asked what they intended to do if they took the ammunition and failed to take the country and hold it, said that they intended to take all they could carry with them and blow the balance up, and retreat in a body to Gen'l Blount's division of the northern army. One man, after making all the confessions about rising in the night, taking the powder, taking the country and holding, and in case of failure, retreating to General Bount's division of the northern army, wound up by saying that when that uprising took place, no man's person or property would be respected if he did not have their sign, pass-word and grip.

When he had concluded this fearful statement, Col. William Young (whom some of the clan killed about ten days afterwards, which will come up in its proper place) said to the man since you and some others who are members of this clan have lived near me, I have been very kind to you all. What was to become of me and my property, for I did not have your sign, pass-word and grip. The man looked at Col. Young for a few seconds and then said, Col. I often thought of you and intended to give you the sign, pass-word and grip before the uprising, that you might save your person and property. But he failed to do so, for the first night to rise had already passed, the heaviest rain I ever saw fall, fell the evening before, and that night, as I shall state when I arrive at that point in my history.

I must give some more confessions. One or two men, after making the confession named in my history, in place of saying as many had done that no man's person or property would be respected who did not have their sign, pass-word and grip, (which was the usual expression), said when that uprising took place, men, women and children of the secession party were to be killed and the property taken and kept.

I was informed by two reliable men that one man said under the gallows (I would not see the hanging) that he was glad this thing had been found out, for if the designs of the clan had been carried out, it would have ruined the country, for the intention was to murder men, women and children of the secession party, and take the property, and he did not want his children raised up under the state of things that this course would bring about. One of my informers told me he wrote this confession down at the time it was made.

By this time we see what the expression that no man's person or property was to be respected who did not have their sign, pass-word and grip meant, particularly with the leaders.

Right here candor and faithfulness as a historian, compel me to state that I am fully and completely satisfied that many of those who were duped, imposed on, and got into this organization, never would have gone into this clan if they had known the dark and bloody intentions of the leaders.

But these men were sworn to obey their leaders if the uprising had taken place. These men would have been with the clan, and the dark designs would have been carried out. Men, women and children would have been killed, and every man in the crowd would have been committed; if they then left the uprisers, they would be killed, and their only chance to escape death would have been to stay with those men. Here I will state about one fourth of these men, claimed to be southern men.

Inasmuch as I have often alluded to uprising in the night, the night having passed and no move having been made, I will here give an account of that night. It was at the breaking up of one of those long dry spells, which is not uncommon in Texas. I had been sending medicine to a case of sickness several days, and about twelve o'clock the man whose wife was sick, came after me, requesting me to go, prepared to stay all night, which I did. It had commenced raining, and by the time we got to the man's house, a distance of about five miles, it was raining very hard and continued to rain till about ten o'clock next day. This was the hardest rain I ever saw fall. This man was one of the clan.

We learned in the jury-room that this night was the night appointed for the rising, and this great and merciful rain, doubtless sent in great mercy came to frustrate the wicked and abominable designs. This night passed before there was any arrests made, or anything known of the existence of the organization by the great mass of the people who were totally unprepared for it.

Here the mind will naturally try to conjecture what the consequences would have been if the rising had taken place that night. How many families would have been made desolate. What wailing and lamentations would have gone up that night. How many who lay down that night with a feeling of security, would have been roused from their sweet slumbers, and before they were fully apprised of their danger, would have been passed into the long sleep of death from which there is no waking, till Gabriel shall give that loud, long and shrill blast which shall reach the great charnel house of death and rouse the nations under ground.

Some may conclude the picture is too highly drawn, but no man can tell what will take place when the blood-thirsty spirit of war rises to boiling heat. Those men would no doubt have fought a dreadful fight, knowing as they would have known that their lives depended on success or a safe retreat. They would have known that no quarters would be given. Some will say they belong to that clan and they never heard of their horrible intentions. You may not have heard it, for I am satisfied there were a good many of the clan who never heard of all these plans, and had no intentions of killing women and children, but knew of the intention to get possession of the ammunition, take the country and hold it, and that could mean nothing but fight, which was proven the first night after the first arrests by those armed men wanting to be led to relieve their friends, and to cap the climax, the members of the clan confessed that they intended to do these things or they would not have told a falsehood which was so much against themselves.

Here I must record a case which occurred when one of the clan was initiating a man: he took the first oath and the first degree, and called for the second degree. The initiator went on to tell him that he must take an oath to do all he could for the north and all he could against the south, he was to endeavor to reinstate the constitution and union, and kill any member who should betray them. Somewhere along here the man who was being initiated, got so mad that he broke loose on the man who was initiating him, and cursed him all over, from the crown of the head to the sole of the foot, and came very near patting it in, and they had a big blow-up, and before they parted, the initiator told him if he told it he would be killed.

While arresting, a squad of men surrounded a house in which there were two men and their wives; the men were supposed to be members of the clan. They ordered a light to be raised in the house, which the inmates refused to do. The squad of men were afraid to go into the house, and the men inside refused to come out and surrender. While the squad of men were maneuvering to arrest the men in the house, there being two doors to the house, each of the men on the inside put a feather-bed on his back and ran out at the door and the squad of men shot at them as they ran. I never learned whether they wounded them or not, for both the men made their escape, and were not arrested afterwards.

I concluded that I ought to give the whole designs of this clan, as they acknowledged themselves, before giving any of the doings of the jury, that the readers might have the whole thing before them, and be more able to form correct conclusions. I suppose no one will now endorse or justify the designs and intentions of these men, as acknowledged by themselves. The only thing to decide is whether or not they ought to have been hung.

In coming to a conclusion in reference to this thing, it would be well to take into consideration that a dreadful war was going on, and like all feuds it brought about an excitement well calculated to impair the mind, dethrone reason, and cause men to do things that in after life, when the excitement had passed away, they will greatly regret.

I have no doubt but both sides regretted much of this thing. Poor old human nature when acting under great excitement is to be pittied. I have heard men say when the war between the states came up, and they went into it, and got the war excitement up, they did things they could not have believed that they ever would have done, but war excitement mastered them.

CHAPTER III

I now begin with the jury, as before stated; the jury met the second day and decided that a majority should rule. Some others and I insisted that it should be unanimous or two-thirds, but the majority rule was established. The excitement had increased. It was terrible with the crowd outside, and no less so in the jury-room. One man, known to be a leader, was brought in and proven to be guilty, he being the man who initiated the two men who had been initiated, and reported to the military. This man was condemned and hung; another was brought and was disposed of the same way, and this was continued till seven were doomed to die likewise. A number of others and I were opposing it with all our powers; I did all the speaking (nearly) but had as well tried to build a dam across Red River in a time of high water with straw, as to resist and control the excitement in the jury-room, and the crowd of soldiers on duty pushed on by influential men. There were eight hundred or a thousand armed men in town by the time the jury condemned seven men.

The crowd were threatening to take the prisoners out and kill all of them. There was a trial made to have me taken off of the jury, because I took the lead in opposing these violent measures. We who opposed hanging insisted to turn the men over to the civil or military authorities instead of hanging, and those not very deep in the thing, to set them at liberty.

The eighth man was tried; he was only slightly in it, but the excitement was so great that he was condemned as readily as the others.

When this was done I concluded that I would stand it no longer; I was determined that I would have a change or leave the jury-room. I rose to my feet and addressed the jury as near as I can recollect as follows: Gentlemen: You are as reckless of human life as though it was a matter of little importance. I am not acquainted with this man, I never saw him till I saw him in the jury-room, consequently my course is not influenced by any particular feelings of partiality. But if you intend to hang all who are no further in this thing than this man is, it is not necessary to do more than bring a man before you and prove him to be slightly connected with this organization and hang him, so you had better pass sentence of death on every man in the prison, for if you continue to carry out the course you have pursued since you came into this jury-room, you will hang all, so you had better dispatch them at once and adjourn. Gentlemen, I have stood this thing as long as I intend to; if there is not a change I will leave. I see in the future the wives of these men in their widowhood, sitting by their fires in the long and lonesome winter nights; the little ones playing around them, the wife looking with a feeling of deep sadness, and casts her eyes on a chair by her side; it is vacant! her eyes are swimming with tears, she is thinking of the dear one, her beloved, the father of her children, and says to herself, where is he? Answer, gone, gone, sleeping the long, long sleep of death, to return to me and my children no more forever. She utters a heavy groan and the sobs of distress escape her lips, ruined, ruined forever, while a flood of tears pour down her cheeks.

And here the tears gushed from my eyes, my heart almost bled. I took my seat.

As soon as I was seated, one of the jurors who had stood shoulder to shoulder with me in opposing the hanging of these men, rose to his feet, took up his hat, and said, he was no longer a member of the jury, and said good bye, and started to the head of the stairs, (we were in an upper room). At this instant two men came rushing to me, one of them caught me by both arms and gave me one of those honest and friendly shakes, which is an indication of deep interest. When this took place the man who had bid the jury good bye, halted. The man who had me by the arms said, for God sake don't break this jury. I asked him why. He said if you break this jury, every man in that prison will be killed before the setting of the sun. The other man who came with him sanctioned what he said. He went on to state that the only chance to save these men, was for the jury to save them, and said he, you can save some. I told them that I knew that the outside proff was strong, but I was not apprised that it was so strong. They told me that I would find it as they had represented it.

I perhaps did as much thinking and planning in a few seconds as I ever did. I knew that if a general slaughter was gone into, unless I made good use of my legs I would go up with the rest, as my course in opposing this wholesale hanging had given great offence. The excitement in the jury-room was of that still and deep character which some times takes place every one waiting in silence to see what would be done.

I said to the two men that approached me: Gentlemen, I yield to your judgment, I will try and arrange this thing.

I then went to the man who had told the jury good bye, and told him what these men had told me, and after a short consultation, we agreed to go back and if the jury would adopt the two-thirds rule, we would act with them, but unless the two-thirds was adopted we would leave. The jury readily adopted the two-thirds rule.

We then gave the man who had been condemned to hang, the benefit of the two-third rule and reversed the sentence of death, by deciding to turn him over to the military authority.

Reader, how does this sound when compared with the ugly tales you have heard about Barrett, in connection with this thing?

If what I have written about my course is disputed, I am prepared to prove all I have said or may say in reference to my course in this thing.

I must now turn to other things which were going on. After we got all that we ever got in reference to the intentions of this clan, it was thought there was something more that had been kept back, and supposing this to be the case, there was considerable anxiety to find it out. A man who was very active against those men came into the jury-room and told us he had a proposition to make. He was told to make it. He referred to a man who was prominent amongst the prisoners, observing that if there was anything kept back, this man knew it, so he proposed to the jury to bring him and tell him if he would reveal every thing, that the jury would release him and release him according to promise, and he would attend to him before he got home. The chairman said, gentlemen, you hear the proposition, have you anything to say?

I waited a short time, and none of the juriors seemed to be disposed to say anything. I rose to my feet and remarked, that I understood the gentleman to mean that in the event we set the man at liberty, he would kill him before he got home, for I could not understand the remark he would attend to him before he got home to mean anything else than that he would kill him before he got home. I paused, and looked at him, for him to correct me if I was wrong. He remained silent, and thus admitted I had came to a correct conclusion.

I asked him if he supposed we were a set of savages, and did he suppose we would accept and agree to his abominable proposition? Then putting my left hand on my right arm between the shoulder and elbow, I told him I would suffer amputation there, rather than agree to such an abominable thing. He then said he withdrew his proposition.

I tell you we had old and hot times.

But I must return.

After we adopted the two-thirds rule, we had some hot contentions in the jury-room, but we either set the men at liberty or decided to send them to the headquarters of the military authorities. When the hanging ceased, and the men were turned over to the military authorities, to be sent there after the jury had completed their work. The excitement increased outside, to give some idea of the excitement, I will state some things that occurred:

There was a man in jail who was charged with being a deserter from the southern army, and a horse thief. As the jury failed to furnish any men to hang, the blood-thirsty men outside took that man and hung him.

As the jury were furnishing none to hang, there was such a strong desire for blood, that the outsiders determined to take all the men in the prison and shoot them. So one evening after supper I was going to the jury-room, and in passing a hotel, a strange man asked me if I was on that jury. I told him I was. He said, you will have nothing to do after to-night. I asked him why? He said all the men in the prison will be taken out to-night and shot. I told him to use his influence to prevent it, as there were men in that prison that the people would not hurt if they knew what I did.

He said it would be done. I went on, and when the jury met, I told them what this man had told me. I said to the jury, we all know that there are men in the prison that it will do to set at liberty, and proposed to them to call up these cases and get as many out as possible, and save as many as we could. They all agreed to my proposition.

So we had a long session that night, and set at liberty about twelve or fifteen.

That same night there were two attempts made to take the men out of the prison and shoot them. The first attempt came very near succeeding. The men formed a line and the head of it marched to the door of the prison and told the door-keeper the jury called for all the men in that room, and all the prisoners but about six were in that room. The door-keeper not suspecting anything wrong unlocked the door and ordered the prisoners to prepare to go to the jury-room. At this time, some of the men seemed as though they were not disposed to carry the thing out, according to the plan adopted, and the leader bawled out with an oath, if you are going to do anything, why don't you be ready.

The door-keeper, supposing what their intentions were, closed the door and locked it. A number of men interposed and pursuaded them to relinquish their designs.

The second attempt was made the same night, as I learned from the door-keeper himself, who is as reliable as any man in the country. A larger number of men marched up to the door of the prison house and demanded the key, but he refused, and they threatened to break the door down. The door-keeper drew his pistol and told them that if they went into that prison, they would go in over his dead body. This brought them to a halt, and after considerable talk and hard words, the men left.

Here the decision of one noble man saved many lives. This man will read this, and remember that awful night. He knows some of my hard places.

I had influenced the jury to adopt the two-thirds rule, which stopped the hanging for a while, consequently the ambition of those who were in favor of hanging, centered on me.

One day I was walking a street alone, and saw a man coming towards me, and on meeting, I readily recognized him to be a desperate character, and a man of influence, a leader in opposition to the prisoners, and I also knew that he had been trying to have me removed from the jury, he having heard me make the speech that I have already named, which speech was made in reference to the eighth man, which caused the jury to adopt the two-thirds rule, and stopped the hanging. I am willing to admit that I would have preferred being in some other place, but I was afraid to turn to another street, considering that I might be shot, for he had a pistol and I had nothing.

We met, and as we met he turned on his heels and pointing to the prison said:

Every man in that prison believes that you are on their side, and are trying to prevent them from being hung, and the people believe it, and they are talking very hard against you; and he told me in an indirect way that if I did not quit, there was danger of me having to go to the elm limb. I acknowledged that I had rather have been in more comfortable quarters. But making a virtue of necessity, and not knowing what this thing would bring about, I became very brave. As a matter of necessity, I tell you reader, I would have made good use of my legs and ran out of it if I could have ran out.

When the jury met that afternoon I laid the case before them, stating the people hearing me speak against hanging, it was calling down a prejudice on me, which I desired to stop, my life being threatened.

I proposed to allow every one who wished to hear all the testimony, but when it came to speaking and voting, to clear the room. This was agreed to and I got along better.

After encountering that man as just named, I was constantly on my guard, and lay every night locked up in a room, as a man and his wife now living in Gainesville will testify if called on.

We must now go back to the jury after we adopted the two-thirds rule: Seven had been hung. When we commenced under the two-thirds rule, we had considerable contention till it was found that this rule would prevent hanging. After that was ascertained we got along quietly and speedily till we got through with all the prisoners on hand, and turned some of them over to the military authorities, the rest being set at liberty.

This brought Saturday evening, and the soldiers were beginning to leave. As the excitement had greatly moderated in the jury-room, we thought it was moderating the same outside, and in order to give it time to moderate still more, we agreed to adjourn for a week and come together the next Saturday and let our decision be known, and I was to make a speech to the people to influence them to abide by our decision, for we were fearful of a mob. Our decision was to be kept secret till the next Saturday. Secrecy was enjoined on all, and we were ready to adjourn.

Some person betrayed us, and told the crowd outside of our decision, and a mob rose and sent two men into the jury-room with word that if we did not give up twenty more to be hung, they would kill every man in the prison.

When this demand came, one of the jurors who acted with me, asked what will you do now? I said the Lord only knows what I ought to do; I have risked my life for six or eight days, and gone as far as I dared to go to prevent hanging. I could contend in the jury-room as I pleased, but cannot war against a regiment of men. I oppose it, but if they take them, they will have to do so, I am not going to say a word.

When I failed to oppose the taking of the men, there was no objection.

I thought when the military failed to protect us and suffered a mob to rise and take these men and hang them, contrary to the decision of the jury, I say, when I thought all this over, I concluded that it was in vain for me to raise my voice against it, so I remained silent. I knew my doom if wholesale killing commenced.

One of these men called for a list of the names of the prisoners. Our clerk handed it to him, and he went over it; took such men as he chose and wrote their names down, then handed the list back to the clerk, and called over the names he had and our clerk marked them out. He then counted his names and he had fourteen. He said as he rose from his seat: I reckon this will satisfy them.

These two men went into the prison, called these fourteen men out, put them in a separate room, and notified them that they must hang next day, which was Sunday.

As soon as these men were gone, I said to the jury: Delay, breeds danger if we undertake to send these men to the headquarters of the military they will not get there, they will be killed. I propose that we meet next Saturday to set all the remaining prisoners at liberty. I told them I did not believe they would be molested, as we had set a good many at liberty, and none of them had been molested.

To this they readily agreed, and passed an order to that effect. I was to make a speech to influence the people to abide by our decision. The jury then adjourned, to meet the next Saturday morning.

I went home that evening, having been absent twelve days and nights. When I arrived at home my wife met me at the gate and asked the news. I attempted to tell her, but my feelings overcame me so, that I choked up and commenced crying. I said I would tell her after I became quiet. And here I will say that no tongue can tell or pen detail what I suffered during those twelve days and nights just closed; not that I had any sympathy for the plans and designs of the organization, for I abhorred and detested their designs. But I considered that it was war times, and as the organization was broken up, all that was necessary was to send them to the military, as the jury at Sherman did, and the county would be relieved.

But I must call the readers attention back to that dreadful Sunday, the day of the hanging of the fourteen men which the mob took from the jury the evening before.

A little after day-light a man road up to my gate and called for me. I at once knew him to be the brother of one of the men to be hung that day. He told me that his brother wanted to see me religiously before he was hung. Reader, this don't look like I had any hand in hanging him. I had been preaching at this man's house.

I told this man to come in, and as soon as we got breakfast I would go with him. He came into the house to wait for breakfast.

Now I am going to depart from my rule adopted not to call names. My reason for breaking this rule is this: There has been more hard things said against me about the hanging of this man than any one that was hung, particularly in his neighborhood. He was a man of good standing in his neighborhood, and was entitled to it, but unfortunately became entangled with this organization, and being a prominent man, the mob in picking these fourteen men picked him.

I was engaged in the practice of medicine, and I did I suppose one-hundred and fifty dollars worth of practice in the families of those men that were hung, and never made a charge. I ate at their tables, and slept in their beds with a feeling of perfect security. I also rode with some of their families in the night. Those near me knew I opposed all that hanging, consequently they had no prejudice against me.

CHAPTER IV

I must now return to the prison. The time for hanging arrived, and I left the prison. I took my seat in a porch at the northeast corner of the square, for I knew that the men would be hauled in a wagon down California street to that old historic tree, which is now dead and lies as still where it has been hauled as the bodies of the men who were hung on its long limbs lie in the grave.

I had not been there long, till I saw the death wagon coming with two of the prisoners. I saw men with guns on each side of the wagon guarding, to prevent escape, and see that the hanging was done, and this was continued till late in the evening before the last one was hung.

As I have nothing to record that took place at the hanging, for I saw no man hung on this or any other day, I will tell some of my reflections as I sat and looked on: I thought of the evening before, when the mob sent and took the men from the jury. I remembered that, though I and others were opposed to letting the men go, we considered the situation too hopeless and fearful to oppose it. But I now saw that we were not apprised of the extent of our fearful surroundings; I saw that the military authorities had detailed men to carry out the designs of the mob. I had expected this thing would be carried out, without regular details. I opened my eyes; I cast about in mind, to unravel this mystery; I thought of the two mobs which rose before in the same night, and both were suppressed by proper exertions, and now the military were carrying out the abominable designs of the mob.

I asked the question: Can it be possible that the military authorities knew that these men were taken from the jury and are being hung, contrary to their decision, or are they in with the mob?

This mystery I could not solve then, and I cannot solve it yet.

Is it not strange that I should have been blamed for not saving these men, when I would have had to contend against such fearful odds, and backed only by the few faithful men (God bless them) who stood firm with me in the jury-room against all hanging? I suppose there were about four or five hundred soldiers in Gainesville at that time. We did all we could to save these men, but that mob defeated us.

There was an order passed that women should not be permitted to be present at the hanging. The women were not noisy, but the signs of deep dispair was manifested by the heaving breast, the falling tears, the heavy groans as though the heart was breaking, and all the vitals of life were giving way. I believe all these men were the heads of a families. The sun set that night on fourteen widowed families, and thirteen families of orphans, for if I recollect right, all these men had children but one.

Language is totally incompetent to express the deep sorrow of that night. Wailing, moaning, weeping and lamentation existed in these families on that dark and fatal night. Tears fell like the rain drop, as tears fall from my eyes at even this distant day, while penning these lines. When the little ones who were just beginning to talk, would say: Ma where is pa? Pa come home, O, ma, go after him. How these words went like a dagger to the heart of that disconsolate wife. He was her husband, she loved him! Let the world say what they may.

I do thank God that I am not guilty of the death of any of those whose death I have just recorded. Neither is the jury, for as I have before stated, the jury had decided to send them to the headquarters of the military authorities in Texas, but that mob took them and hung them. As I have already stated the jury had decided to adjourn for a week, when they came together the next Saturday to set the remaining prisoners at liberty.

During this week of adjournment, I went to town every day, and the excitement was moderating, and everything bidding fair for a favorable condition on the next Saturday, the day the jury was to meet.

About the middle of the week, when I got into town I was met with the startling news that a man by the name of Dickson, who was a citizen of Gainesville, had been killed in the brakes of Red River by a squad of men belonging to that organization. This revived the excitement to a flame. I walked in amongst the soldiers; I could hear threats of clearing up the prison that night.

Several, including myself, commenced pursuading them not to do that, for there were men in the prison that were only slightly in this thing, and we continued to pursuade all day, but seemingly to little effect. Late in the evening the talk was that they would clear the prison that night.

I went home that evening with a gloomy feeling, and during the night when I awoke, I listened for the report of guns, but heard none. I was up next morning very early, and went to town, and learned that the prisoners had not been interrupted, but heard the horrible news that Col. Young had been killed by that clan.

The excitement was fearful. Men were swearing they would kill every man in the prison that night. I availed myself of every opportunity that presented itself to pursuade them not to murder the prisoners, but I was compelled to be very humble, in order to effect anything, and finally came down to hard begging.

Late that evening I went home, feeling the prisoners would be murdered that night, and I expected any minute to hear the horrifying report of the death warning guns, but that awful sound failed to reach my ears. When I arrived in town next morning, learned to my great satisfaction, that the prisoners had not been molested.

Here I must state that all the time that this thing was going on, occasionally men who were in this clan, were coming in and surrendering, and some of them had been hung.

I had frequently sent word to those men who were on the dodge, to leave the country and stay away till the war closed, and things settled down, and not come to Gainesville, for we had too many already.

A number had taken my advice and left the country, but some were still lying in the brush, bent on mischief, and they killed Dickson and Young, and no doubt would have killed more if they could. Although I opposed the hanging, I was then and am now bitterly opposed to the designs of that clan. But I thought then and yet think that to extend mercy, after breaking up that organization, was the best course to pursue, and I am proud to record that some of the men who were in this organization who were set at liberty, are good, peaceable and quiet citizens.

I must now give the particulars of the killing of Dickson and Young, as I learned from them the men who were by their sides when they were killed.

Dickson and two other men were in the brakes of Red River hunting deer, when they saw a man on horseback at the edge of a thicket. This man rode into the thicket. They followed him, Dickson and one man riding beside each other and the other man about one-hundred yards behind. When Dickson and the other man got to the edge of the thicket, Dickson was shot and fell from his horse, and the other man thought he was shot at and missed. When this occurred, the man who was riding by Dickson's side turned his horse, rode to the other man and told him to go to Gainesville and report what had taken place, and said he would go to the settlement on the river and get assistance and come to Dickson's relief. The man who went to the settlement on the river, went to Col. Young's and told him what had occurred and told him to gather all the men he could, telling Young where to find Dickson. This man gathered a small squad of men and went to where Dickson fell and found him dead and lying on his back with his arms lying across his breast and his gun lying across him, showing that the men who killed him had been there. He was taken to his family.

We now turn to Col. Young and his squad. They went in search of Dickson, but failed to find him. They went down a hill which placed them in a position to be seen from a flat at the foot of the hill. When they got to the foot of the hill, in crossing a ravine they were out of sight from the flat a short distance, but in crossing a ridge Young was a little before the man who was riding by his side. When he got so he could see over the flat, he spoke out, saying: Here they are boys, supposing that they had found the men who had gone to Dickson, when he saw men; at that instant he was shot, the ball entering his head above the right eye. He, in falling, held to his bridle reins, which suddenly turned his horse around and pushed the horse on which the man by his side was riding into a gully out of sight. This perhaps saved the life of that man.

The men dismounted, expecting a fight, but after waiting awhile and no attack being made, they crowded to the top of the small ridge and looked over the flat and saw no enemy. They sent for a wagon to take Young home and he died before they got him there.

Two men had been killed the same day, and no one knew how many were in the brush nor to what extent this thing would be carried.

The excitement boiled over. Our horizon, in reference to this matter was dark and gloomy; the situation was fearful; I could discern the signs of the gathering storm by the expressions of the crowd, such as the following:

The fight has commenced and every one we turned loose is ading that much to the strength of that clan.

Others would say with an oath that every one of them ought to be hung. We will clean them up to-night.

The condition was like the sound of many waters or the fearful mutterings of the gathering storm. No man knew but what he might be the next victim. No man knows to what extent the excitement went, unless he went amongst the crowd for days as I did, and heard them talk. I considered the situation such that I had better quit begging for these men, so I spent my time in walking through the crowd and hearing them talk, expecting every night the prison would be cleared, but it was not.

Saturday morning came, the day for the jury to meet, and when the roll was called, two of the jurors who had opposed the hanging were absent, and their places filled with men who failed to act on the moderate side.

The first thing the jury did, was to reconsider the decision of the jury to set these men at liberty when they met this morning.

This decision was rejected, which placed the prisoners on trial the same as though they had not been tried.

The excitement had reached the jury-room. I and a few others saw the situation at once. The testimony against the men on which they had been tried was all written down, consequently there was nothing to be done but read it, and take the vote. One was put on trial the vote taken and he condemned to hang; a second was disposed of in the same manner. I made a trial to stop the course of things, but I saw that it was useless to make any attempt to save the men by a vote. I then proposed a compromise: I proposed to allow them to select six of the worst ones and hang them, and set the rest at liberty. I saw they were going to hang a good many more than that, and I was striving to save as many as possible, but the jury rejected my proposition. When they rejected it, hope fled, and I took my seat to watch the course of events. I sat sad and silent till six were condemned and not one set at liberty, for it was hang or set at liberty.

The seventh one was put on trial, his was quite a moderate case, and some defended him. While they were talking on his case, they would look at me as though they wanted to say: help us. I thought now is the time to effect something.

I rose to my feet and addressed the jury about in these words: Gentlemen, I have remained silent, and suffered you to take your own course without interruption, but in this moderate case, I would with due respect, ask the question, if it would not be better to set these moderate cases at liberty, and if you must have blood, take the worst cases? We took the vote and set the man at liberty.

I saw that a reaction, to some extent, was taking place in the minds of some of the jury, and right here the day's fight commenced.

I did all I could to save the men, and those with whom I voted came up nobly to the work, and our side gained regularly. After we commenced setting some at liberty, we succeeded in saving about two-thirds.

This was the hardest day's work I ever did, or ever saw done. A portion of the men with whom I acted, contended manfully against all hanging, while others sometimes voted against the men.

This condition of things caused the fight to be fierce, each party striving to get those who sometimes voted for the men, who held the balance of power, and the party that got them, carried their point.

The present condition of things was well calculated to cause the contention to be of the fiercest character. Everything was done and said by each party that it was thought would cause them to succeed. As for myself, I know that I never exerted myself to the same extent as I did that day.

In speaking against the hanging, I said everything I could think of, that I thought would prevent hanging.

I can give substantially my speeches that day. I told the jury what I had often said to them before, that they were laboring under an excitement which had unhinged their minds. You think you are doing right, but said I, when the war closes and the excitement passes away, and you calmly look back on the course you are now pursuing, for you are bound to come to these sober hours of reflection, you will be astonished that you were so excited as to think that you were doing right. When you come to this, you will then say Barrett was right. All of those jurors that I talked with afterwards came to this sober conclusion.

Reader, the writer, who opposed this hanging, is the man whom you have so often heard was one of the leaders in this hanging. Most of the things I have written can be proven by living witnesses.

Now let us come to the result of this day's work.

There were nineteen men condemned to be hung; the balance, about fifty or sixty, were set at liberty.

These nineteen men were hung in consequence of the killing of Dickson and Young. If they had not been killed, all of these men would have been set at liberty that Saturday morning.

The prisoners condemned, were notified that they were to hang next day.

CHAPTER V

Here I must notice the joy and sadness of that Saturday. The jury had decided the Saturday before to set all these men at liberty this Saturday. This decision was known by the wives and friends of the prisoners, and they came that morning with glad hearts, prepared to take their loved ones home with them.

But ah! what must have been the feelings of that wife, when she was informed that her husband had to stand another trial, and at last, late in evening, the horrible news revealed to her, that after all, he had been one of those unfortunate victims, condemned to hang the next day. Others had to await the decision of the jury. But I was told that when one was set at liberty, the wife or friends, or both, took them and left Gainesville in haste, rejoicing, while those who got news that the husband was to be hung, were following or before, weeping, while wailing and lamentations burst from their lips.

In some houses, sadness and deep sorrow reigned supreme. None but those who experienced that dreadful night can fully realize the deep sorrow of loving and disconsolate hearts.

But that dreadful Sunday dawned, and I went to Gainesville, not to see the men hung, for I would not see any of those men hung; but I went to see how the things which were going on would terminate. I took my seat in the same porch at the northeast corner of the square, where I sat when the fourteen men passed which the mob took from the jury and hung.

The hanging did not commence very early, and when the last one was hung, the sun was low.

When I started home, my nearest way was to go so as to pass within twenty feet of the tree on which the men were hung, but I took the next street north, to keep from seeing any man hanging.

This day closed this thing, which had caused such an upheaving and excitement for the last twenty or twenty-five days.

There were forty hung, and two who broke from the guard were shot and killed, making forty-two deaths.

If I was to stop my history here, I am apprised that the reader would be disappointed, and desire to know what were the consequences resulting from this dreadful affair. This desire shall be gratified, as far as a statement of facts will do it.

This organization having been broken up, everything seemed to quiet down, but there was fears that the friends of those men might seek revenge, consequently every man connected with this thing was on the lookout day and night. But no revenge was taken.

I remained at my home, three miles east of Gainesville, about one year. I was in danger all the time from two sources, first, from a few persons who entertained a deadly hatred against me for assisting to set so many of these men at liberty. I dreaded them. Second, I dreaded the families and friends of those who were hung, being ignorant of my course, so I was between two axes. Some of the families of those who were hung treated me with a birth of friendship, surpassing what they had done before.

While this was the situation, the military authorities formed a frontier regiment, and the most of these men were going into it.

I said to my wife, when these get together in the army, there will be a great deal more danger than now.

I determined to leave the county, and in a hurried manner, moved to Mt. Vernon, Titus county, now the county town of the new county of Franklin. I shall continue my case after awhile.

When the war closed and the civil courts were established under Governor Hamilton, the grand-jury found a bill against all the jurors.

But before the grand-jury found the bill, the Federal soldiers came in and such running and taking to the brush, had never been in Cooke county; not only the jury, but a good many others who had taken an active part in that hanging.

But when the jurors who were in Cooke county learned that they could be tried by the civil authorities, they came in and surrendered. Some of the jurors were not in the county. I, for one, was not here.

These men were all tried and acquitted, but their lawyers fees were heavy, particularly when the hush-money was added to it. Perhaps some of my readers may ask what does hush-money mean? It means money paid to lawyers to prevent them from appearing against the persons on trial in court. I state this, as I received it from some of the men who paid the hush-money. This, the hush money business, was named to me when my trial was pending. I remarked that I did not intend to pay any hush-money, and if any lawyer appeared against me because I would not pay him hush-money I would make him sick and tired of it before he was done with it. But none appeared.

I am apprised that in this last sentence I am anticipating, but as the hush-money business had come up, I would finish it here, and drop back to the thread of my history.

My own case must now come up in detail, and particularly so because nearly every man in any way connected with that thing had been lost sight of but me, and in many cases people in Gainesville were prejudiced against me, and thought I was the ring leader in that thing, and they did not know the name of any other juror or any other person connected with it. This I found out by asking them if they knew who else beside me was on that jury; their answer was, they did not know the name of any other jurors. This will all be explained in its proper place.

As I have already stated I moved to Mt. Vernon in about a year after the hanging, which was in the fall of 1863. I remained there till June 1865, when I moved to Bell county. The war having ended, everything was in a foment and I became satisfied the federal soldiers would come in to arrest men. I knew they would get my name as one of the jury at Gainesville, for I had many acquaintances in Bell and Williamson counties who knew I was on that jury, but did not know whether I was opposed to that hanging or not.

Being satisfied my name would be given as one to be arrested, I went to see the county judge, as I knew he would control the arrests. I had a long private interview with him and told him my situation. He told me that the federal soldiers were coming in to arrest men, and if they got my name as one of the jurors in the Gainesville affair, they would arrest me. But he promised me that he would not report me. I told him if they got my name and were aiming to arrest me, to give them this proposition from me.

That, if the proper officer would bind himself officially, that I should have a fair trial at Gainesville, and, also bind himself that when we got to Gainesville that if I wanted a witness who was on the dodge, he would permit me to send for such witnesses and the witnesses should be secure from arrest for twenty-four hours after concluding his testimony, I could meet him at Gainesville any day he might appoint, but I would not be arrested; and if he was not willing to take my word, he might draw a bond for one-hundred thousand dollars and I would get signers enough to make it a good bond; but I never heard of this any more. And from an interview I had with the judge afterwards I was satisfied I would be reported.

I commenced making every preparation to meet the storm when it came. I put out my sentinels in order or know what was going on, expecting every day to have to take the brush to prepare for leaving the country, and I had but ten dollars to travel on.

At this time of distress Chilton A. Andrews, whom I had known almost from his cradle, came to my house, and when I told him that I was expecting to have to leave the country, he asked me if I had money to travel on? I told him I had ten dollars only, and I had been trying to sell property for money, but could not, but if I had to leave the country, when my money gave out I would sell my horse and take it afoot.

He handed me thirty dollars, for which I feel grateful while writing these lines.

Not long after this, one of my sentinels came to my house one night after dark; he told me he left Belton late that evening and he stated that about two o'clock that evening fifty federals came into Belton, and late in the evening forty of them put on their overcoats and got on their horses and rode out of town. He went into where the others were and asked where those men were? They said they did not know. When he received this answer he was satisfied that they were going to arrest men, so he came to let me know what was on hand.

When he was done, I said to my wife: this is enough, bring me some blankets. She brought them and I made for a thicket about one-quarter of a mile from the house that it was difficult for a man to walk through. I selected my place and made my bed, but I needed no bed because I could not sleep.

I employed my time in listening for the tramp of horse's feet, and standing in the edge of the thicket to hear anything in the road, which was but a short distance from me. I heard the dogs bark at a house not far from mine; I supposed the soldiers were there, and I learned afterwards that they were there at that time.

In a short space of time I heard the barking of dogs at a house on a hill not far off. I afterwards learned that the soldiers surrounded this house while the man was asleep, roused him up and took him a prisoner.

Morning came, and my son came and told me that there had not been any soldiers at my house. I told him to keep a sharp lookout and if nothing occurred to prevent, I would be in for breakfast.

This was my first night in the brush, but not the last by a good many.

I went near enough to the house to see everything, and went in for breakfast. After breakfast I went into a thicket and slept till dinner, after dinner I sent one of my sons to Belton to get the news. He returned and brought news that the federal soldiers had arrested seven men the night before. This made me feel quite skittish. I told my son to bring our horses to a certain place in the brush and I would go to Brooksville, in Williamson county and he could stop at Salado, as he had business there next day.

We started, and, worked our way to Salado, evading the public road as much as possible, and arrived there about midnight. I had a good friend keeping hotel in Salado whom I wanted to consult.

We waked him up, and when I told him my plans, he told me I had too many acquaintances there, but to go back home and wait till he brought me word, and he would arrange a safe place for me.

While we were planning, my son went out, but returned immediately and informed me that a squad of soldiers were coming. Not to be out done my plans were arranged. I took a stand in the dining room door, which led to the kitchen; intending if they came in, to go into the horse lot and get after Dick for not putting up our horses; they were hitched at the fence and the moon shining bright, and when I got in the lot, to leap the fence and make for the brush.

But I saw them ride by and go to another tavern. I then went into the brush, leaving word so my son could find me.

In about an hour, the soldiers having left, he came to me and I directed him to bring my horse and to meet me at a noted live oak tree in a thicket the next day and bring me some provision, for I would have nothing to eat till he came.

But here I must turn my attention to what was going on at home.

The soldiers came to my house the night I was at Salado. Two of them rode up to the gate and got off their horses. We had some fierce dogs. My wife went to the door, drove the dogs off and the men came near the door and asked if that was where Dr. Barrett lived? She told them it was. They said they were sent to arrest him. She told them I was not at home. They said their orders were to search the house. She told them to come in, and lighting a candle, took them into every room. When they had finished their seach, they took seats before the fire, and by this time others had rode up to the gate. She walked out and invited them to come in and warm. She asked the men if they had met with their supper? They said they had. She told them if they had any inclination to eat, she could soon cook it.

They thanked her and left, and they never came to my house any more.

Let us now return to Salado.

My son brought me my horse and started back for the brush, near home, a distance of a nine miles. I arrived within about a quarter of a mile of home, stripped my horse and turned him loose, knowing he would go up for his feed. He went up, and then my son came home, about twelve o'clock, and relieved my family.

About two o'clock my son brought me provision and appointed the time and place for the next meeting and left. I had settled down on the plan not to go into my house and I never went into that house any more.

That evening after my son left, it clouded and had the appearance of rain; I gathered a quantity of chunks to make a place to stand on in the event it should rain. I knew that by standing on my chunks under an uncommon large fork of the tree with a blanket I could keep from getting much wet.

About dark it commenced raining slowly. I heard a noise as I thought like something scraping the leaves. I looked in the direction of the noise and I could see a dark spot. I began to think I knew there were catamounts and panthers in these thickets. I supposed it was a panther, I thought of moving, but I was satisfied if it was a panther, that it would follow me and I did not like to give up my good shelter from the rain. I was satisfied that if it was a wild animal, a fight was inevitable. I concluded that I would rather bring on the fight than wait to be attacked; so I felt about amongst my chunks for as sound a one as I could find and walked slowly till I got within about five steps of my panther and I made a charge and struck with all my power, when lo and behold I hit an old stump. Right there I took a hearty laugh, and I sometimes laugh yet when I think of this circumstance.

After my encounter with my panther (stump), on examination I discovered the noise in the leaves was caused by the water falling from a tree that had lodged in falling. The rain ceased and it snowed a little. I began to feel drowsy. I warmed up by jumping up and down till sufficiently warm. I lay down on the chunks and used the root of the tree for my pillow, and in this way I got several hours sleep. I had matches with me, but was afraid to make a fire. I had started in to beat the federal soldiers, and I adopted the plan to run no risk that I could avoid.

This was the first of January, 1866, pretty cold weather to lay in the brush without fire. The soldiers were scouring the country, and I was in a strange country and did not know who to trust and I had to depend on myself, and one old-time friend who was of great service to me.

I passed my time as well as I could in my situation. I built a fire two nights, but I became fearful that the fires might lead to my arrest, and I built no more fires, as the weather was not very cold.

The time arrived for the meeting with my son. We met in one of those dense thickets, so common in that region. He brought me plenty of provisions and a bottle of wine made out of the Mustang grape. I made a hearty meal, and sat down to wait for night to go where I intended to camp.

The sun set, and as soon as it began to get dark, I worked my way to a fence not far off, which was my guide to the hollow I intended to camp in. I walked in the trail by the fence, almost afraid of the noise of my own shoes, while I stepped the light and cautious step of the savage. When I got to the corner of the fence, there was a very public settlement road run near the corner of the fence—this road I had to cross to reach the timber in the hollow that I intended to camp in. It was open prairie from the corner of the fence to the timber.

I stood at the corner of that fence a short time, and concluded to run across the road to the timber. When I got to the road, I looked to my right and saw a squad of soldiers. I knew it to be soldiers, by a white horse, which I had understood one rode. When I saw this, I was running at about half speed and knew they could cut me off from the brush, but I could reach the fence before they could catch me; so I turned and made for the fence, and as this was no place for half speed, I called up my strength and let loose all my running gear and did the best running of my life till I reached the fence. After I got over the fence I ran some distance and stopped to look back and listen; and as I could not see or hear anything, I sat down to take a rest. I have no means of knowing whether they saw me or not. But this I do know, they gave me an awful scare. By the time I got rested, I was very thirsty, and having no disposition to go over the ground where I had been in such a tight place, I concluded to go to the Leon river which was near the other side of the field which I was in to get water-melon and wait for the moon to rise. I worked my way to the river, got water, walked to the root of a large tree near the road, and sat down to wait for the moon to rise. While sitting there, my thoughts were busy. I thought of having to leave Cooke county in consequence of being in danger from a few who were hostile at me for preventing so many of those men from being hung; and also from those who were hostile against me for the hanging of these men, who did not know that I opposed that hanging.

Thus, having been run by both sides, I was now being chased by the federals, and being certain that if the federal authorities knew the truth of this matter, they would bless me. I thought it very hard to be chased by both parties.

While thus engaged, a man came riding along the road, singing merrily. I thought, happy man. What would I give to be as happy as you seem to be, with no storm-cloud hanging over you with its threatening dark and dangerous mutterings. But the future in my case was dark and gloomy, uncertain and unsettled.

While thus musing, I went into a sound sleep. Sweet messenger of temporary peace when the mind is relieved of anxiety, care, and forebodings of danger.

When I roused up the moon was about two hours high. Having adopted the rule to avoid being near roads in day-light, I now worked my way to as safe a place as I could. I remained there until my old-time friend sent the word to come to his tan-yard, in Williamson county; about twenty-five miles from my house. I had lain in the brush night and day near my house for ten or twelve days and nights, and had a fire two nights. The federals still scouring the country and arresting and sending the prisoners to Austin, and putting them in a loathsome, lousy, dirty prison. If I could have been assured that I would have a trial before the civil authorities, I would have surrendered at once. But the intention of the authorities at Austin was to try all who were taken there by a military court.

I was determined that I would not be tried by a court martial, composed of men, some of whom would not stay away from a bottle of whisky an hour longer than usual to save a man's life.

The intention to try everything by a court martial will come up more fully in the progress of my history.

The time to get to my friend came, and my son and I started in the night with one horse to keep down suspicion. We expected to get there before day, but we failed, and arrived there early next morning. There were two tan-yards, one shoe-shop and a saddler shop, situated at the edge of a level piece of ground of about eight acres, with two branches running through it and surrounded by hills and as good a thicket as heart could wish to hide in. I got into the thicket without any one knowing it but my friend.

Here I will state why I went there.

We became suspicious that my house was watched, so I went to my friend and my son to put out the report that I was gone to Mexico. During the time I remained here I had as good a time as I could have expected, under the circumstances. All the annoyances I had were from wood rats and pole-cats. They came so near me some times that they would wake me, and I had to knock the bushes to drive them off. At last I made the discovery that the bones which were brought in my meat and dropped near where I slept, drew them. I gathered all the bones and took them about thirty steps, and kept a regular bone-yard and was relieved. My old-time friend was called off on business, and he got one of his hands to attend to me. This was the only man that knew I was there.

My heart swells with gratitude to these men while I write, and if they should ever read these lines, I want them to know that I have not forgotten them, and as long as I retain my senses all the ravages of time can never erase the pleasing recollection of their every kindness.

After I had been there some time, I learned that preparations were being made to try every man that had done any thing during the war, by a court martial. When I heard this, I decided to leave the state and not return until the civil authority gained the ascendency.

I sent word to my son to come to me and bring only one horse, to avoid suspicion. He came, and my good wife sent me plenty of provision, such as biscuit, pound-cake, beef, and a bottle of wine. My two friends came with him in the night to where I was. We had a general talk; and when we counted the time, we made out that I had been there in the brush eighteen days and nights, and was at the fire one time. I also learned from my old-time friend that there were seventy-four men in prison at Austin and they were still bringing them in. They were all to be tried by courts martial.

Here I must digress for awhile from the regular thread of my history, and tell what I learned from undoubted authority. There was an extensive monied arrangement on hand that, if it had been carried out, would have put into the pockets of a few men thousands of dollars. The arrangement seemed to be this:

There was a lawyer there ready to defend these men for a large fee, and I learned from one man who was turned out, that he and his father were in prison, and they paid this attorney five hundred dollars each. He said the most of the prisoners employed him, but he did not know how many paid him. When this splendid monied arrangement only wanted authority from the commanding officer of the district of Louisiana and Texas to complete it, when application was made to him for authority to establish this court martial, which was to pour thousands of dollars into the pockets of the men who were managing this thing. Be it said to his everlasting honor, he, with his usual nobleness of soul, refused to grant the power to establish a court martial to try these men, but he sent and had them all set at liberty, thus disappointing and thwarting the abominable designs of those men. I have been told there was a mighty shaking amongst the dry bones in Austin when this refusal came, and instead of giving authority to establish a court martial to try these men, the order came to set them at liberty.

The condition of these men in their disappointment, reminds me of a certain lawyer who was noted for crying when speaking on a criminal case: It was supposed that if five hundred dollars were laid down and he was told that if he would talk himself into a cry over it, he should have it, the supposition was he would make the tears come.

If these men did not talk themselves into a cry because they slipped up on this splendid money scheme, I would not be surprised if they grieved over it until they made the water flow freely.

But I must turn back to the thread of my history.

My son having come to take me near home to prepare for leaving the state, I gave my two friends a hearty shake of the hand and we started about eight o'clock. It was a dark, drizzly night, and twenty-five miles to make before day, and only one horse. We had to travel the public road most of the way and were in danger of meeting federal soldiers at any minute. I walked most of the time by the side of the horse, holding to the blanket, with the understanding if we met the soldiers, he was to ride so as to cause them to pass on the side opposite from me, if they halted him to stop and give his name and if they inquired for me, to tell them I was on the dodge for fear of the federals, and I was to slip out of the road and he to ride on, and after going far enough to keep down suspicion he was to wait for me, and if anything took place to separate us, we were to meet the next day at my live oak tree, where I thought I had encountered a panther, as I have already stated. But nothing occurred that night worth naming until we came to the crossing of the Lampasas, a small river. Here the road enters the channel going north, but turning to the east, running down the channel on a gravelly bar. There was a good spring that broke out of the bank a little before we crossed the stream. When I got into the channel of the river I looked ahead and saw two tents near the spring, and three wagon sheets on the other side of the stream.

I called my son's attention to the tents and wagons. He asked me what it meant. I told him we were in a federal camp. He asked me what we would do. I walked out before him and in a voice loud enough to be heard at the tents and wagons, asked him if he thought we would get to Belton in time to see those men we wished to see. He said he supposed we would if we got along as fast as we had since we started. I remarked that we must be there before day, for the men would start by day-light, and we must see them. By this time we had passed the tents and were ready to cross the river which was low and shallow. I said to him: Ride up to this bank and I will get up behind you and cross the river.

When we reached the other side we were near the wagons. I got down and told my son to give me the bottle we had to carry water in. I filled it and took a drink, and then filled it and gave him a drink, then filled it again and told him to put it in his pocket, stating we would get no water fit to drink till we got to Belton. Then went on without being molested.

I did not expect they were accustomed to stopping men on the highway, but I knew if we acted in a suspicious way it would cause our arrest, and I intended to outgeneral them. I met with a man afterwards who told me that he and others were prisoners there that night. We reached the brush near my home a little before day that morning.

By this time the reader may ask why I did not come to Gainesville and fare as those other jurors did.

The reason I did not come to Gainesville, I first learned from a source that I was sure was reliable, that the federal soldiers were in Cooke county, and when the citizens got a chance they attacked them and cleaned them up. I was determined that I would not go into such abominable work as that. I also learned that those jurors who were in Cooke county had given themselves up to the civil authorities, and the military authorities had taken them out of the hands of the civil authorities and were going to try them by court martial.

When I heard this, I was determined to stay away until I could have a trial in the civil courts—which I did, but I afterwards learned that my information was false.

I now must return to the thread of my history.

I lay in the brush near home about two days and nights, while preparations were being made for me to leave the country. The necessary preparations having been completed, I started for north Mt. Pleasant, Marshall county, Mississippi, about 9 o'clock in the night, January 2....th, 1866.

I went through Tyler. Passed the stockade where many prisoners were kept during the war, and saw where those who died while prisoners were buried. I felt sad. I thought: Poor men died far from home far from wife, children and friends. Some of whom yet feel sad when they think of the dear ones who are sleeping the long sleep of death in a far off and strange land. Gone! gone! to return no more forever. Who can number the wailings and lamentations that went up in consequence of those who were killed and those that died in that unfortunate war?

I thought of my own situation; exiled from home, and the future dark and uncertain, and war the cause of it.

Here let me record that I have a read a great deal of war history, and at an early period in my life I became opposed to war. Am yet opposed to it. Who can measure the tears that have been shed in consequence of the dreadful casualties of war?

If all the tears which war has caused to flow could be collected together, they would form an ocean sufficient to swim the living.

When will the nations of the earth beat their swords into plow-shears, and their spears into prunning hooks and learn war no more?

Not until that blessed day comes.

Lord, hasten that day.

But returning from this digression, I pursued my journey until I got near Dangerfield. Not having money enough for my long journey, I concluded to call on my friend, T. H. Turner, for money, knowing that he would assist me if it was in his power. When I got there he was gone to New Orleans to lay in goods. I made my condition known to his blessed wife, (and would say God bless her, but I have no doubt but He has already blessed her, for she is dead). She told me that her husband had taken all the money that was in the store when he left, but sent and got all the money there was in the store and went into her trunks and got the last dime on the place, and when counted she had sixty dollars in specie. I had only asked for fifty.

While I write my heart swells with gratitude to this blessed woman.

I now felt safe, having plenty of money to last me until I could reach my former friends in Mississippi and Tennessee, whom I knew would supply my wants when I reached them.

Having been thus fortunate I pursued my journey. I got along very well. When I reached the edge of the Mississippi bottom, I was told it was forty miles to the river. I was frequently in mud and water and had much difficulty, but finally reached a ferry on the river early in the day, but the wind was so high that I had to wait for it to cease.

About one o'clock the wind had sufficiently calmed for the boat to cross, as the ferryman thought. So we started, but before we got to the middle of the river, the wind set in worse than ever. The waves rattled and the boat rocked. I began to think that here my career would probably end, and I made all the preparations I could to be ready if the boat should capsize. I laid off my coat and boots and arranged my horse for swimming and waited for the result. My legs trembled and my knees smote together. I called the attention of the man who steered the boat to my trembling and said to him: I am a man of strong nerve, and never in life have I been situated where I trembled as I do now. But at last we got behind a point in calmer water and made the shore in safety. When we landed and were safe, one of the heaviest loads I ever had on me fell off and I felt vastly better.

I was advised at this ferry to go up the river about one hundred miles to Frear's Point and then cross the bottom. I was told that the direct route to Holly Springs ran so near the Chatahoochie river that it would be very difficult for me to get along.

Having crossed the river safely, I started for Frear's Point and arrived there without much difficulty. My route was on the levy part of the time, the balance in the roads crossing the bends. When I got to Frear's Point, I learned it was thirty miles across the bottom. I struck out through mud and water and some snow, and safely reached the hills and felt much relieved, as I had surmounted the great difficulty and soon reached the Holly Springs—about fifty miles from north Mt. Pleasant, my destination. And on February 16th, 1866, as I learn from my journal which I kept, I arrived at north Mt. Pleasant.

Here I met with my brother and his wife, whom I had not seen for thirty-three years. We had been separated so long they did not know me. Here I learned that my brothers' son, C. C. Barrett, was in the printing office at Holly Springs. After staying with my brother a few days, and informing him of my situation, and getting him to watch the signs of the times for me, he being a lawyer, he had good opportunities to watch for me. My rule was when I stopped to put out my sentinels. Men were being arrested by telegraph.

Having completed this arrangement, I went to Holly Springs and informed my nephew of my situation, and got him to save the Texas papers which he got in exchange and watch for me. I returned to north Mt. Pleasant to rest, for I felt that I was almost worn out. While here resting I had ample time for reflection.

Here I shall make quotations from my journal I kept at the time:

Here I am exiled from home and not knowing when, if ever, I will be permitted to return.

An innocent man thus driven from home while some of those most guilty men are unmolested, but as frequently occurs, the innocent suffer while the guilty go unpunished. I thought of the upheaving in our government, the unsettled state of the public mind. The minds of a large portion of the people seemed to be unhinged and reason dethroned. The political horizon dark and gloomy, uncertain and unsettled, with scarce a ray of light penetrating the darkness. There I saw President Johnson's amnesty proclamation which was, I thought, a ray of light to direct the mind to hope. While at Holly Springs, I saw more of the destructive ravages of war. It was here that General Van Dorn burnt out the supplies of General Grant, and compelled him to abandon the plan of attacking Vicksburg by land and forced him to return to Memphis and attack by way of the Mississippi river.

The court-house and more than half the houses on the square were in ruins.

I went back to north Mt. Pleasant; started from here the 23d day of April 1866; sold my horse and took the cars at Lafayette depot for Giles county, Tennessee, where I was raised. I arrived at Campbell's station Saturday, three miles from brother Wade Barrett's and had a rejociing meeting. After staying with my brother some time, visiting and receiving visits from my old friends, I went to Franklin, in Williamson county, where I had some relatives. While here, I visited the battle-ground where General Hood had that destructive battle with the federals. I also went to the McGavoc cemetery, where most of the confederate dead had been buried. The dead of each state, as far as known, were buried together.

Here I quote from my journal:

I arrived at the McGavoc cemetery and walked through the city of the dead. I am now seated on the graves of the Texas dead writing. I thought, poor fellows. You died far from home. Far from the dear objects of your affections. You have fought your last battle. The fierce conflict has passed away and the roar of the cannon has ceased the noise, and shouts of battle is no more heard. But, who can point out the scenes that transpired during that dreadful night after the battle?

It is hard to die in the midst of kind friends, surrounded by all that kind hands can do, but these had no wife, father, mother, sister, daughter or son to speak words of comfort, or give a cup of water to quench their dying thirst.

While they lay weltering in their blood the tide of life slowly ebbing, surrounded by the shriek of the wounded and groans of the dying, thinking of the loved ones far away at home without the least prospect of ever embracing them again. They must struggle in all the agonies of dissolving nature on the bloody field, with thoughts on the loved ones at home, and weeping as life became extinct.

The affecting scenes which transpired on that dreadful field will never be revealed to mortals on this earth. If angels ever weep they must have wept while viewing that awful and bloody battle field that night. What a comment on the depravity of man?

After the roar of battle ceased, what a wailing of sorrow went up all over the land, north and south, as the sad tidings were conveyed to the homes of the slain. How sad the wife, the father, the mother, the brother, the daughter and the sister!

And now, when the family circle is formed, there will be one vacant chair. They will miss him. Oh, the sad horrors of war. The heart sickens, the tears fall while I write.

There is more than fourteen hundred of the confederate dead who have been interred and buried in this cemetery and not done yet. What a city of the dead!

How still they sleep! Revolution may follow revolution and change the face of nature; the cannon may roar, the battle may rage with all its fierceness, the wounded may shriek, the dying may groan, they heed it not, they sleep on. Nothing but Gabriel's trumpet can wake them.

My heart is filled with gladness to be assured that there is a bright and glorious region in the deep and mysterious creation of Him who inhabits eternity. Where there is no cannon roars, where there are no shrieks of wounded or groans of the dying; where the silence of the midnight hours are never broken by the wailing sons and daughters of sorrow telling their grief to the trees of the forest; where none of those heart-rendering scenes can come.

This blessed region is that house not made with hands, eternal in the heavens; where He who sits upon the circle of the heavens is the center of praise and directs the rejoicing of that happy throng.

Reader, please excuse me for keeping you so long on this battle ground and cemetery. I have only quoted a little from my journal of what I wrote while there. This belongs to my history, as I promised to give some of the consequences following that affair at Gainesville. Also I was anxious to record my opposition to war.

Now we travel a little faster.

I went to my brothers' in Giles county, Tennessee, August 1st, 1866. Here I received some letters from Texas. I thought of returning home, but the cholera was raging in Nashville and on the rivers.

As I could not start home, I yielded to the strong solicitations to preach, and spent all my time in preaching until November the 13th, 1866, at which time I took the cars for home.

At Memphis I boarded a steam boat and traveled to Jefferson. From Jefferson, I traveled by hack and horse-back to my home in Cooke county, Texas, near Gainesville, December 12th, 1866. Having been away from my family eleven months and fifteen days, the reader can imagine the joy of that meeting for I can not write it.

Here I ought to state that my wife had sold out in Bell county and gone back to Cooke.

Having arrived at home, my friends seemed glad to see me. Those who were so bitter against me for defending those prisoners—the excitement having passed away and reason returned—all met me with warmth of friendship, having seen their error. Some of the worst ones are now telling they acted with me. Now they say (as I told them they would say when the excitement passed away) Barrett was right

Passing over many false statements made against me, one falsehood was so glaring that I must tell what it was. A man who did as much against those men who were hung as any man who was in any way connected with that affair, took my position and told that I occupied his position (which was a bad one), and this report he put in circulation after I moved from the county. I did not hear of this report until I got back.

This falsehood shows the bitter feeling against me for opposing the violent mesures that were carried out on that occasion.

Perhaps I have written enough at the present about misrepresentation.

I can not say good-bye for there is nothing good about falsehoods. But I can say a dry adieu.

Having arrived at home, I set about having a trial, but it took about two years to get it. When my trial came up it was the poorest thing of the kind I ever saw. The district attorney had two witnesses. He examined one and turned him over to the attorneys. They asked no questions, but told him to stand aside. The second witness was disposed of in the same way. The district attorney asked my attorneys what they wanted to do with the case? They said they wanted the verdict of the jury. The case was given to the jury without pleading. The jury sat in the jury box, and the foreman said: "Write on that indictment, not guilty," and I was discharged. I thought if ever the mountain of labor brought forth a mouse, we had it in this case about which there had been such a splutter.

As soon as my trial was over, and I obtained such a complete and clear acquittal, I concluded that in the future I might have a use for a certificate, as the judge and lawyers would sign.

The time has come that I have use for that certificate and here it is:

"State of Texas, county of Cooke—this is to certify that Rev. Thomas Barrett, of the state and county aforesaid, was tried at the December term of the district court for Cooke county, Texas, on the 5th day of December, A. D. 1868, and honorably acquitted by the jury, there being no evidence against him, and the jury returning instantly a verdict of not guilty."

Witness our hands on the 11th day of December, A. D. 1868

(Signed)

HARDIN HART, Judge of the 7th Judicial District
J. W. THROCKMORTON, Late Governor of Texas
W. T. G. WEAVER, Late Judge of the 7th Judicial Dis't.

When the above certificate was handed to me, I saw that it failed to state what I was tried for. I called Judge Weaver's attention to the omission, and he gave me the following:

P.S.—The trial referred to above, which took place on the 5th day of December, A.D. 1868, was upon an indictment found against Dr. Thomas Barrett and others for the illegal hanging of forty men in Gainesville during the confederate war. Given under my hand and signed,

W. T. G. WEAVER

The above is positive evidence that I voluntarily met the indictment against me, and not a particle of evidence could be produced against me. I was prepared with witnesses in the court-house to prove that I took the course in the jury room that I have stated in this history, but my legal counsel declined introducing it because there was nothing to contend with.

Kind reader, in as much as my course in reference to that hanging has been misrepresented more than twenty-two years, and my character having been greatly injured, by the many falsehoods put in circulation against me, I say, kind reader, permit me to introduce one more witness, which will be my last. The witness I allude to is Judge P. T. Andrews, of Grayson county, who died in the spring of 1866. Judge Andrews and myself became acquainted in Missouri in the spring of 1843. I boarded with him nearly a year. We moved to Texas the same year, I think. He came on a visit to my house in 1862. When he arrived at my house I was in Gainesville on that jury. He came to Gainesville and was in the jury room the most of the time for two days, and when he learned that I was in a difficult situation, he voluntarily wrote me a letter, and now hear what he says:

SHERMAN, Texas, January 26th, 1866

DR. THOS. BARRETT:—

Dear Sir—Having some idea of your peculiar situation, I feel it my duty to address you this note that you may know, so far as I am able to inform you how I viewed and understood the peculiar situation in which you and some others were placed in in that trying and most unfortunate period in Cooke county while the rebellion was going on; when men ran mad like mustangs; when almost all men had run mad and forced everything before them. (Of course I allude to the unfortunate affair in Gainesville). I recollect well, you remarked to me (privately) soon after my arrival in Gainesville, that you would not be on the jury for a thousand dollars, but would not have refused for all you were worth, and even more. My understanding from you was that the pressure was so great and the spirit of blood so high, that had you refused, you endangered your life. Moreover, I can say, as I have frequently said, that I was permitted in the jury-room; I was proud to see and hear from there that you was a check on that bloodthirsty body, and was convinced that had you been absent, they would have done much more mischief than they did.

During my stay in Gainesville, I kept cool and had perfect control of myself, and could look on the infuriated mob of more than five hundred rough men in arms. I went home to Sherman, and found that the spirit and excitement had reached my county. When they organized, I was chosen as one of twenty-four jurors. What should I do? I thought of you, and after deliberating one night, I got my consent to serve. I feel now that a few of us were able to keep the blood-thirsty spirit in check till reason could prevail and save our county. But, my dear friend, we did not have such bloodthirsty spirits as you had in Cooke. I believe while in Cooke, and told you so, that some of your jury was acting badly. You agreed with me. And so far as I saw, or heard, you was a check to all that hanging. I am proud that I know as much of you as I do. I have known you for many years, and have seen you in hard places, in prosperity and adversity, but have never known you to flinch from duty.

Now, you are at liberty to show this to whom you please, and I here say that these remarks have not been asked for by you; they are a free-will offering, because I believed it to be my duty to make them. Should you ever be molested I will try to be present if necessary.

[Signed] P T ANDREWS.

This testimony is clear and unmistakable, as far as Judge Andrews saw, and the credibility of his testimony can never be successfully impeached by mortal man. I could get many certificates from others who were in the jury room at different times; all stating that when they were in the jury room I was opposing the violent measures which were gone into in that affair.

I suppose I have said enough on this part of the subject, but if any one disputes the correctness of my history let them open the ball and I will face the music.

CONCLUSION

I suppose by this time some of my readers are anxious to know how I have been able to write this history in detail twenty-two years after the thing occurred. I feel entirely able to give the necessary information, and in answer to that, I have forgotten very few things during my life, which made a strong impression on my mind at the time they occurred, and while writing this history, as I write the things that I have written came up in regular order as if it had been only a short time since they occurred. I have an extraordinary recollection, as I could give examples which would astonish the reader, as it has often astonished me, but it is not necessary here.

Another reason is, since the occurrence of that affair a great many of my friends have asked me about that affair, and I have gone over all that I have written and more many times—not all at one time, but one part at a time and another part at another time—and this was continued through a period of twenty-two years, and now I am nearly done writing it.

Another reason for being able to write it out in detail is, I wrote out a good deal of this thing not long after it occurred. This and my journal which I kept when I went to Mississippi and Tennessee assisted my memory. So by aid of these I have been able to give this thing in detail to give a full understanding of this unfortunate affair.

When I determined to write this history, I studied long and hard to adopt the best plan, and after mature deliberation I settled down on the plan pursued, to begin at the beginning and tell the working of this thing in the jury room and outside, and as far as possible cause this affair to pass before the mind of the reader as it would if he had been present and seen and heard all as I did. How far I have succeeded in this undertaking is left for the reader to determine himself.

As I have already stated elsewhere in this history, I have given the circumstances but suppressed names so as to leave every man as far as possible where he is now, for I have no enemies to punish.

There is another strange thing about this affair: The curious reader wishes to know why it is (as I have stated) that almost every man who was connected in any way with that thing had been lost sight of but myself, and it is said I was one of the leaders in that hanging.

When I found out that this condition of that thing existed to a considerable extent against me, I was at a loss to understand why it was; but I was determined to unravel the mystery, so I employed a few friends to investigate this matter and report to me, and the information received from them in addition to what I knew myself I was soon able to satisfy myself why it was so, and here it is:

I was a public man—a doctor and a preacher—and an old settler near Gainesville, and supposed to have some standing (easy brother) in the community.

This is the way the thing has been conducted. There has been for some years past a large increase to the population of Gainesville and many of the newcomers must see that old historic tree, that old elm, and they must know something of that hanging, and when told very imperfectly of it they oppose it, and a few justified and defended it, and those defending it were hard pressed for arguments, so they would refer to me, saying: "There is old man Barrett, supposed to be a good man and a man of high standing in the community, who was one of the leaders in that hanging." They had no intention to injure me, but used my name solely for the purpose of carrying out their point in trying to justify that hanging. While I do not charge them with intending to injure, yet their course injured me as much as if they had been doing all they could against me.

But the misrepresentation being once started it was passed from one to another, and a falsehood once started has no stopping place, and one man can circulate more falsehood than twenty men can head off and correct.

This thing was used by a few of the baser sort against me, and they raised great opposition to me religiously.

But in taking leave of this part of my history, I must say that although this thing has and is injuring me, there are very few who had any intention to injure me. But after it was stated many believed it, and being prejudiced against me told it to others and in this way the falsehood was kept up and circulated by those who could not, if they had known the truth, been influenced to take any hand in circulating as base a falsehood as this was.

I have no enemies to punish, no malice against any one. I forgive all as I hope to be forgiven.

In this concluding chapter, I must state that it has been a matter of much regret that I felt compelled to allude to my course so often, but know no way so likely to set me right before the world where my history is read as the course I have pursued.

And I think the reader will agree with me when I tell him myself and many others have been trying to correct the misrepresentations against me, and at this present time while I am writing, it is, I suppose, injuring me ten times as much as it did twenty years ago, having passed over almost every one else and settled on me with all its fury.

Many persons who are strongly prejudiced against me, in consequence of that hanging, if they were asked who else were connected with that thing could not give another name. But a great number know I was connected with this affair and a great many think I was a leader in it.

Almost everywhere I go I find this thing has gone before me, and went there unfavorably. I heard of it in Cincinnati, and one of my friends was good enough to set me right, but his opportunities being limited could do but little.

Heretofore, those who knew that I was badly misrepresented had nothing that was decisive, but when this history is circulated, as it will be, there will be something permanent to refer to, as I have made my course public and defy successful contradiction. The people of the United States, so far as this history is read, will learn the truth. The universal idea (almost) as I have before stated, has been that they were hung because they were union men, which this shows was not true.

I am not so vain as to suppose that I have made no mistakes, but I am vain enough, if you call it vanity, to be sure I have made no mistake in any important matter.

After I arrived home at the conclusion of my long run-a-way, I made a calculation of what I was injured, and I never could make it less than three thousand dollars. A serious loss for an old man of limited means.

In this concluding chapter, I repeat what I have stated elsewhere, that almost everything that I have stated can be proven by living witnesses.

THE END

George Washington Diamond's Account of the Great Hanging at Gainesville, 1862

A PUBLICATION OF
THE TEXAS STATE HISTORICAL ASSOCIATION

Printed in the United States of America
Austin, 1963
The Texas State Historical Association

George Washington Diamond

(1835-1911)

George Washington Diamond's Account of the Great Hanging at Gainesville, 1862

EDITED BY

SAM ACHESON

AND

JULIE ANN HUDSON O'CONNELL

Austin, Texas

THE TEXAS STATE HISTORICAL ASSOCIATION

1963

*Foreword**

A UNIONIST "PEACE PARTY PLOT" aimed at revolt against the Confederate government in Texas was discovered in September, 1862, in the North Texas area including Cooke, Grayson, Wise, Denton, and Collin counties. Prompt action by local authorities broke up the organization in October, 1862. Following a declaration of martial law in Cooke County, a "Citizens Court," or jury, of twelve men composed of army officers and civilians was formed at Gainesville. It found thirty-nine of the participants guilty and sentenced them to be hanged for conspiracy and insurrection. Three other prisoners who were members of military units were permitted trial by court martial as they requested and were subsequently hanged by its order.

Since that time the only reliable and lengthy account of the awesome event has been the one written by a member of the jury, Thomas Barrett, *The Great Hanging at Gainesville, Cooke County, Texas, October, A. D. 1862* (Gainesville, 1885). An extremely rare item of Texana, it was reprinted in 1961 by the Texas State Historical Association.

Soon after the "Great Hanging," George Washington Diamond, a newspaper editor and publisher of Henderson, who had joined the Confederate Army, took leave from his regiment, the 3rd Texas Cavalry, to visit in Cooke County where his brother, James J. Diamond, lieutenant colonel of the 11th Texas Cavalry, had assisted in the discovery of the conspiracy. George W. Diamond was asked by his brother and other members of the Gainesville court to write a full account of the "Peace Party Plot" and the trials of the conspirators. The original records of the court were turned over to him to be used as the basis of his chronicle. Shortly after the end of the Civil War, he began this account, the final draft

*The editors wish to express their appreciation for the assistance and counsel in editing the manuscript of members of the Diamond family and of H. Bailey Carroll. They also wish to thank Kathryn S. Hughes and Ruth Harris of Dallas for transcribing the manuscript for publication. Full responsibility for all decisions and interpretations of textual matters in the editing is assumed by the editors. The author's sentence structure and punctuation have been carefully preserved.

of which was completed, as internal evidence indicates, sometime between February 1, 1874, and December 20, 1876. Diamond was then living at Whitesboro, Grayson County, where he died in 1911.

Since Diamond's death, the unpublished manuscript in his handwriting has remained in the custody of his heirs. Its existence was made known recently by a granddaughter, Mrs. Harry Harlan of Dallas. Because of the author's intent expressed in the manuscript to lay his compilation before the bar of history, Mr. and Mrs. Harlan have allowed the work to be edited for publication. By reason of its generous detail, it is a valuable complementary piece to the Barrett account.

Behind the Great Hanging at Gainesville lies a sequence of events and movements—local, state, and in the broadest sphere of the nation itself—that bear significantly upon its occurrence. They were the same developments that had led already to the secession of Texas and other Southern states, the formation of the Confederacy, and the outbreak of war between North and South.

As early as the annexation of Texas to the Union in 1845, the state and its people had become embroiled directly in the bitter intersectional disputes then raging over the question of slavery. But it was not until the late 1850's that the area of North Texas in which Gainesville and Cooke County lay became a battleground in the preliminaries to armed conflict. The reason for this delay is indicated largely by the character and background of most of its inhabitants at the time.

The settlers in this isolated, frontier region of Texas were mainly small farmers and mechanics, most of them drawn from Kentucky, Illinois, Indiana, Tennessee, Missouri, and other border states by the lure of free land to Texas. Few of them owned any Negro slaves. Most were indifferent, or even opposed, to the institution of slavery. Cooke County was only one of some ten or eleven contiguous counties settled in whole or in part by persons with the same general background. The counties comprised what had long been known as the Forks of the Trinity (River) area. Measuring roughly one hundred miles square, it extended southward from the Red River to a line below the cities of Dallas and Fort Worth. There was also settled within it a small but forceful minority with differing background and outlook. These persons had come chiefly from the longer settled areas of eastern Texas or from states in the Deep South. They tended to prefer land in the rich bottoms of the main river courses rather than in the open prairie country. Their farms were basically cotton plantations. This minority group owned almost all of the Negro slaves introduced into the area, and it was as strongly pro-Southern in sentiment as any group of Mississippi or Georgia cotton planters.

Viewed nationally, it was obvious that the opening of the Territory of Kansas to white settlement in the 1850's had produced a bloodstained rehearsal of civil war itself. Reverberations of that struggle between Free-Soil partisans and Abolitionists on the one hand and pro-slavery, extreme state's rights men on the other were felt sharply in North Texas. The people in the northernmost counties of Cooke, Montague, Grayson, and Fannin were closer, in fact, to the bleeding ground of Kansas than to their own state capital at Austin. Little more than two hundred miles of Indian Territory, present Oklahoma, separated them from the fratricidal strife to the north.

Reflections in North Texas of the troubles in Kansas were confined at first to nonviolent contests for the minds of inhabitants. The principal threat, in the eyes of the pro-Southern extremists, was found in the Abolitionist evangels from beyond the state. Most of these were itinerant preachers of various denominations who urged an end to slavery on moral or religious grounds. Ministers of the Methodist Episcopal Church, by then referred to as the Northern Methodist Church, were especially suspect. The northern counties of Texas also were the only part of the state in which this parent branch of American Methodism insisted upon maintaining a conference, or organization of local churches, in the face of objections from the younger Methodist Episcopal Church, South.

The contest on a statewide scale between pro-slavery extremists and die-hard Unionists in Texas remained primarily political as expressed at the ballot box. But it reached a new high in 1859 when Sam Houston as the champion of Union and the Constitution defeated Hardin R. Runnels' bid for a second term as governor. Houston had no more solid support than in the North Texas counties, whose people felt that his victory at the polls largely had settled the question of Texas taking part in any rift of the Union.

But pro-slavery leaders in the North Texas area by that time felt goaded to register their sentiments outside the polling booths. In April of 1859 the annual conference of the Northern Methodist Church embracing northern Texas met on Brushy Creek in Fannin County. A mass meeting held simultaneously in the county seat of Bonham denounced the conference. Several hundred members then proceeded by horseback the five miles to the conference meeting. There the mob forced the Reverend Anthony Bewley, chief minister on the Texas mission, and other delegates including the presiding bishop, to disperse. The churchmen were warned that blood would flow if they continued their ministry in Texas. The temper of the pro-slavery men was inflamed further the same year when John Brown staged his raid on Harper's Ferry in Virginia some months later.

It was the presidential contest of 1860, though, that hastened a showdown in the long intersectional dispute. The ill-fated Democratic National Convention, meeting at Charleston that spring, split hopelessly over the selection of national standard bearers, thus opening the way to victory for nominees of the recently formed Republican Party. The Republican nomination of Abraham Lincoln for president was taken as a direct challenge to Southern secessionists, a turn viewed with the gravest concern by pro-Southern leaders in North Texas.

In the interval between Lincoln's nomination and his election in November, 1860, public opinion in North Texas was greatly agitated by an unexplained civil commotion. Early in the afternoon of Sunday, July 8, a series of fires broke out at almost the same moment in Dallas, Denton, Pilot Point, Waxahachie, Kaufman, and several other towns in North Texas. No one knew, or would admit, who started the blazes. The economic loss, particularly in Dallas where the fire got beyond control, was heavy.

Although Governor Houston minimized the importance of the fires, pro-Southern leaders of the area pointed to them as part of a projected slave uprising planned and fostered, it was charged, by Abolitionist preachers. At Dallas a vigilante committee of fifty-two tried and hanged three Negro slaves accused of complicity. At Fort Worth, another mob captured and hanged the Reverend Anthony Bewley, following discovery of a letter purporting to link the presiding elder of the Northern Methodist Church with a secret order, referred to as the Red Circle. The order was said to be dedicated to the extinction of Texas slave owners and their followers.

Lincoln's election in November led to demands for immediate secession in Texas and other Southern states, but the firm Unionist stand by Governor Houston delayed the issue from coming to a head in Texas until February 23, 1861. On that date, a statewide referendum was held on an ordinance adopted by the state secession convention at Austin to sever the union of Texas with the United States. James J. Diamond was one of Cooke County's three delegates to that convention. He also was named a member of the convention's Committee of Public Safety which, during a six-weeks' recess of the convention, became in effect the revolutionary government of Texas. Through its agents and armed forces, it compelled the surrender of all United States troops and forts in the state even before the statewide vote on secession was taken.

Although Texas as a whole voted for secession by a margin of 46,129 to 14,697 ballots, nineteen of the 122 organized counties cast majorities against it. Eight of these opposing counties were in North Texas, including Cooke County, which voted 221 to 137 against withdrawing from the Union. Grayson, Collin, Montague, Fannin, Wise, Jack, and Lamar counties also rejected the ordinance of secession. But Dallas, where the worst of the fires of the previous year had occurred, voted by a margin of 741 to 237 votes for secession. Tarrant County, in which Bewley had been executed at Fort Worth, followed the lead of Dallas by a vote of 462 to 127.

In spite of this split among the counties in the Forks of the Trinity area, public opinion appeared to be unified there in support of the Confederacy, once the two sections of the nation were plunged into war. Notwithstanding the heavy registration of opposition to secession in Cooke and adjoining counties, most of the men of fighting age rallied to the armed defense of their state and the Confederacy. Many of those who had been most pronounced against secession took up arms against the Union.

After the firing upon Fort Sumter in April, 1861, the state government at Austin moved to put Texas on a war footing. In

May, Colonel William C. Young, a veteran of the Mexican War and a Cooke County planter living in the Sivil's Bend area along the Red River, was ordered to raise a regiment of 1,000 men from ten North Texas counties, including Cooke, Grayson, Collin, and Denton counties. Designated for the protection of the northern border, Young's 11th Texas Cavalry moved shortly into the Indian country to capture the United States outposts of Forts Washita, Cobb, and Arbuckle, thus becoming the occupying force that held the area between Kansas and Texas.

By December, 1861, the Texas legislature passed a general act providing for the internal security of the state. Thirty-three brigade districts were created by the act. District Number 1 comprised Cooke, Montague, Wise, Denton, Jack, and thirteen other north and northwestern counties, with headquarters at Gainesville. As commanding officer of the district, William Hudson, a forty-year-old native of South Carolina and a longtime resident in Cooke County, was appointed brigadier general.

It is significant that although Confederate state authorities took for granted that North Texans were united in loyalty to the new government, the military units raised in the area were officered primarily by those with long-held Southern sentiments. This policy extended from the commanding general at Gainesville through the companies raised in each county. Thus in and from Cooke County were such undoubted Southern spokesmen as Hudson, William C. Young, James J. Diamond, James G. Bourland, the aging Daniel Montague's son-in-law, William C. Twitty, and others equally reliable in strategic command of military units in the area.

It is against this background of events and movements that the "Peace Party Plot" was discovered and acted upon in the fall of 1862. In writing his account of the Great Hanging, George W. Diamond sought to justify the establishment of the court and the severity of its judgments. In his mind, as in those of members of the court who aided him in the preparation of his narrative, the "Citizens Court" was not an extra-legal viligante group, or mob, but an orderly constituted body which acted with regard for due process of law in carrying out its frightful duty. In this, the Diamond account differs markedly in tenor from the account written some ten years later by Thomas Barrett, with which the reader may compare it profitably.

INTRODUCTION

In introducing the following pages to those who may wish to read them, the writer[1] deems some explanations necessary in order that the stirring scenes therein detailed may be properly understood and the design of their publication appreciated by an unbiased, discriminating public.

Immediately after the adjournment of the "Citizens Court," and after the return of the writer then on leave of absence from the army, [he] was placed in possession of all the records of the tribunal whose judgments and verdict had sent more souls to eternity in a shorter period of time than ever known before to modern civilization. Before the adjournment of the court, a committee was appointed by it to take charge of these records, for

[1]George Washington Diamond, newspaper editor, lawyer, and author of this document, was born to James and Nancy Diamond in De Kalb County, Georgia, on December 26, 1835. After his graduation in 1857 from Albany University (presently New York University), with a law degree, he followed five brothers to Texas. They were James J. Diamond, John R. Diamond, and William W. Diamond, who settled in Grayson and Cooke counties and Greene Diamond and Eli Franklyn Diamond, who lived in other parts of the state. George W. Diamond located first in Rusk County, where he became a partner in the publication of the Henderson *Times,* previously the *East Texas Times.*

At the outbreak of the Civil War, George W. Diamond sold his interest in the newspaper at Henderson and joined Captain R. H. Cumby's Company B, 3rd Texas Cavalry Regiment, as a private on May 7, 1861. He saw service in the initial phases of the war in Missouri under General Ben McCulloch. On leave from his unit late in 1862, he visited his brother James J. Diamond in Cooke County shortly after the events described in this narrative. Garland Roscoe Farmer, *The Realm of Rusk County* (Henderson, 1951), 50, 130.

Subsequently, George W. Diamond was transferred to the 11th Texas Cavalry, of which his brother James J. Diamond was colonel. In the spring of 1863 he raised a cavalry company on the lower Brazos River and served as a captain in Terrell's Texas Cavalry Regiment. He fought with this unit in the battles of Mansfield and Pleasant Hill, Louisiana, on April 8-9, 1864, in which Confederate forces turned back Major General Nathaniel P. Banks' Red River campaign, the last Union attempt to invade Texas.

Returning to Henderson at the end of hostilities, George W. Diamond was elected state representative from the district embracing Rusk County in the 11th Texas Legislature. Because of the military reconstruction of Texas, this body was not permitted to convene until 1870. Meanwhile, George W. Diamond moved with his family to Whitesboro, Grayson County, where he continued to make his home until his death on June 24, 1911. He practiced law in the county seat of Sherman during Reconstruction, held several public offices in the county, and was a member of the staff of the Whitesboro *News.*

the purpose of preserving them and so disposing of them that the history of its transactions might be perpetuated and justice done to those who participated in its deliberations.

The writer, at the urgent solicitations of this committee, compiled the following memoranda from those records; and in obedience to the request of the "Court," there expressed, they are now[2] offered to the public as a just vindication of the conduct of those whose acts have been the subject of unjust criticism from one end of this broad land to the other.

After arranging those records in the form in which they are here submitted, the committee assembled all the members of the court, and after a careful reading and examination gave them their unanimous and unqualified approval. It was left discretionary with the writer as to the proper time for their publication.

During the war it was not regarded wise or proper to further inflame the minds of a people already swayed by the passions and prejudices, incident to a gigantic, internecine struggle for sectional supremacy by the publication of a work calculated to further impress them with the wrongs and injustices which they conceived had been inflicted upon them. And the publication being to some extent political in its character, it has not been deemed prudent or politic to circulate it among a people engaged in a mutual struggle to heal the wounds and quiet the passions engendered by a long and bloody war.

But now since peace and quiet has been restored, all the states having resumed their constitutional relations to the genl. govt., and the people all united again as in a common brotherhood pledged to a faithful allegiance to the national flag, the publication of these pages may be regarded as a duty this writer owes to unwritten history to offer them to the future important historians of this country north and south, who may deal with the facts

---

[2]In spite of Diamond's expectation of early publication, his compilation of "memoranda" was not committed to print during his lifetime, or later. It may be presumed that the state of local public feeling in the decades immediately following the end of the Civil War did not encourage it. The reception of another account, published in 1885 by the Reverend Thomas Barrett, a member of the "Citizens Court," may have been part of the deterrent. Thomas Barrett, *The Great Hanging at Gainesville, Cooke County, Texas A. D. 1862* (Gainesville, 1885; reprint, Austin, 1961).

Since the author's death more than half a century ago, his manuscript has been preserved by members of his family, who feel that it should be made available at last in print to "an unbiased, discriminating public."

contained in them upon a broader and more comprehensive scale, submitting them to a wider and more universal circulation for the opinion and candid judgment of Mankind.

The only merit the writer claims for his work is its *unvarnished truth*. It only contains the *actual proceedings* of the "Court," with the letters, confessions, speeches and military operations of those engaged & essentially connected with it, without any attempt on the part of the writer to warp the text to suit his own taste or to attract the reader.

It being a truthful statement of all the circumstances connected with the exciting scenes enacted on that bloody theatre, the writer appeals to those who may differ with him in opinion, as well as those whose friends or relatives may have died upon that fatal limb, if it is anything but justice to them that the whole truth should be published so that, as before stated, an impartial public might correctly judge between the right and the wrong. Hundreds yet live to attest the truth of what is herein detailed; and being thus fortified, the writer challenges denial or evasion on the part of any one who may desire to question any important or material statement herein contained.

Those who participated in the events of that period believed then, and believe yet, that under all the circumstances they did but their duty to themselves and their families. None regretted the necessity of their action more than themselves; and having herein made known to the world all the facts which governed them in the discharge of their solemn duty, they rest their case and will patiently abide the decision of a generous public.

ORIGIN OF THE ORDER

Early in the year 1858, after the organization and establishment of the "Overland Mail"[3] through Texas, people of every shade of opinion and men guilty of every species of crime began to pour into the State from all quarters of the globe.

This magnificent enterprise that reached "from the rivers to the ends of the earth" entered the State in Grayson County on the north and passed beyond her western boundary at El Paso. With St. Louis as the great north-western depot, immigration teamed into Northern Texas by this line to an extent hitherto unknown. So rapid was this influx of a heterogeneous population that in a short time the character of the citizenship in Cooke and Grayson counties was materially changed. Until that time this section was thinly settled, with a quiet, hardy, industrious population which had not been excited and disturbed by political divisions and discussions. This sudden and rushing tide caused alarm among the older inhabitants; not because they did not desire immigration; but because the actions and conduct of so many strangers in their midst created suspicions and fears that the interests of the old class would not harmonize with the new.

This increasing volume of immigration continued until the question of secession became open for discussion and after the people, with great unanimity, pronounced for the right of secession, immigration in a great measure ceased. And finally, upon the suspension of the Overland, and the withdrawal of the coaches and stock belonging to the Company, many of those who had

---

[3]John Butterfield's Southern Overland Mail Route between St. Louis, Missouri, and San Francisco, California, began operation on September 15, 1858. It continued as a contract mail, express, and passenger stage line operating across Northern Texas until March 1, 1861. It entered Texas by way of Colbert's Ferry on the Red River eight miles east of Preston Bend. It ran fifteen miles south to Sherman, thence fifteen miles west to its next relay point, Diamond's Station (the homeplace of John R. Diamond, one mile west of present-day Whitesboro, Grayson County). Its third relay point was Gainesville, seventeen miles to the west in Cooke County, from whence it continued by way of Jacksboro, present-day Graham, and other points in West Texas to El Paso and on to the Pacific coast. Rupert N. Richardson, "Some Details of the Southern Overland Mail," *Southwestern Historical Quarterly*, XXIX, 1-18.

come to Texas under its auspices returned to the North, taking with them their property and families.

But many of those who remained seemed to be restless and adventurous in their dispositions, manifesting an unfriendly spirit toward the older settlers. This produced its natural result, and in a short time mutual distrust and dislike, criminations and recriminations characterized the intercourse between the two parties. And it may be truly said also that many who had resided for several years in this section of the state, from the South as well as the North, espoused the cause of theft, rapine and murder, and became leaders and helpers in their wicked crusade against the peace, the property and the lives of good citizens.

It would, therefore, be unjust as well as untrue, in fact, to charge the crimes of the order to the population of any one section of the country. The political sentiments of the immigrant from the North, no doubt, had much to do in stimulating and urging forward the daring and impulsive desperado from the South. The bold denunciation of the act of secession by the Northern immigrants, also by a small class of the Southern people, was the foundation upon which unscrupulous men bent on ruin and plunder based their criminal conduct.

They used this political sentiment, openly advocated, as a pretext for their movements, and instead of entertaining a moment's thought or care for the "Union," or its perpetuity, they rejoiced that the general disturbance and confusion had given them an opportunity to gratify their revenge against a neighbor and sordid lust for plunder.

These two classes readily formed an alliance, offensive and defensive and, as the sequel will show, began a regular system of robbery, rapine and murder unparalleled in the history of this country. It is no good or sound argument to say that they only killed a few men in the course of their proceedings, and that, therefore, the punishment of their crimes was too severe, too summary in character and too extensive.

It may be answered by the confessions of many of them as their dying declarations that they intended to kill *all* the people in this section, and when the Northern army came in, they would be quieted in their titles to the homesteads of those killed and driven from the state.

They expected this result as the legitimate tendency of their zealous cooperation and harmonious action with the invading armies of the North which, they supposed, would reward their fidelity to the flag of the nation by a system of confiscation and agrarianism, which too often, as history shows, attends the triumphs of the conquer[or] over the conquered. Their own voluntary confessions prove this beyond dispute.

Many of those engaged and belonging to the "Order,"[4] some tried and found guilty, some acquitted, and others who fled the country, came from the State of Kansas, where but a few years before no doubt they had been engaged in the domestic troubles of that Territory. And it appears from their operations in Texas that they designed in the outset to form a nucleus around which might gather from all sources and all parties a body of sufficient power and influence to produce a like degree of domestic violence in the section which had but recently given way to legitimate and organized government in that state.

Many who participated in the operation of the "Order," and nearly all the leaders, came to the section but a few years or months previous to the organization; and though coming from different quarters, there appeared to exist a congenial sentiment between them from their first acquaintance, which finally resulted in a combined movement for the accomplishment of the objects hereafter detailed.

And but for the prompt and decisive action of the people in thwarting their design, it may reasonably be supposed that the scenes of Kansas would have been reenacted on Texas soil. The people of this section viewed with great alarm the dangerous tendency of a concentration of this class of citizenship in their midst, and very wisely determined to adopt the necessary measures to avert the mischief designed to be inflicted upon them.

---

[4]The group of Union sympathizers in Cooke and other North Texas counties, banded together in behalf of the restoration of the Federal Union, are referred to variously by Diamond as the "Order," "Organization," and "Institution." This Yankee underground, or resistance group, may have been an outgrowth, in part, of the secret Abolitionist group active in North Texas in 1858-1860.

EFFECTS UPON THE PEOPLE

In pursuance of a general understanding to watch their movements, nothing was said or done on either side to disturb quiet and peaceable relations between the two parties. The "Order" had committed no acts of violence, or made any demonstrations indicating its objects, aims & future policy of its operations. Thus matters rested, each party watching and suspicious of the other, until the final disruption of the Union and war had become a reality.

Many of the states had seceded from the General Government and declared themselves free and sovereign in their own right. And it will be remembered by Texans that after many of the states had passed ordinances of Secession, and secession had become a fixed fact, Texas, through her delegates in Convention assembled, submitted a like ordinance for the ratification by the people of the state;[5] and that simultaneously with the discussion upon the subject, and before the day selected for the vote on the ordinance, a proposition emanated from some of the North Western counties, through a Sherman newspaper[6] strongly favor-

---

[5]The Secession Convention of Texas met in Austin on January 28, 1861, and two days later submitted an ordinance to repeal the annexation ordinance of 1845 for approval or rejection by the voters of Texas. The statewide election was set for February 23, 1861, the ordinance to become effective on March 2, if the referendum was favorable to it. E. W. Winkler (ed.), *Journal of the Secession Convention of Texas, 1861* (Austin, 1912).

[6]The Sherman *Patriot* was the principal Whig newspaper in North Texas during the 1850's, with the exception of Charles DeMorse's *Northern Standard* at Clarksville. It strongly opposed the secession of Texas. Graham Landrum, *Grayson County, An Illustrated History of Grayson County, Texas* (Fort Worth, 1960), 24-25.

No copy of any detailed "proposition" to organize a separate state in North Texas is extant, although such action was foreshadowed in a document dated January 15, 1861, at Austin on the eve of the Secession Convention of Texas. Said to have been issued from "the Unionist ring at Austin," that document was widely circulated in Collin and other North Texas counties and published in the *Southern Intelligencer* (Austin), January 31, 1861. It served notice that if the then approaching state convention should disregard "the wishes of the Conservative Union men of the State of Texas, and especially the Northern portion of the state," by declaring the State of Texas out of the Union "without submitting their action to the people of Texas for ratification at the ballot box," Union men were resolved "as a *dernier resort* to make an effort to unite a sufficient number of the northern counties into a state, and make application at the proper time for

ing, and earnestly recommending the organization of a new state. This scheme seems to have been the result of mature reflection and calm deliberations, as the meets [*sic*] and bounds of the new state were properly & systematically designated, embracing quite a respectable portion of the state.

The paper in which this proposition had its practical origin was published by one Capt. Foster,[7] who was notorious for his hostility to the Southern people, and who was afterwards killed by some unknown persons in the streets of Sherman.

From whence this proposition originally came, it is not deemed necessary to inquire. If the project was ever entertained in good faith by any good men, it certainly was a most unfortunate stroke of policy at that particular time and particular locality chosen for the accomplishment of such a purpose. The scheme was a bold one, openly advocated and seriously recommended to the confidence and support of the people.

No doubt its advocates at that particular time resorted to it to attract the attention of the people from the important question then pending—the adoption of the ordinance of Secession—and by not committing themselves to the policy of secession and resistance to the General Government, they would more readily command the aid of that government in their scheme to cut themselves loose and establish their new state by violence and the bayonet, as was done in the case of West Virginia.

It certainly did accomplish much in the way of neutralizing and allaying the enthusiasm in favor of secession, though it signally failed to effect the general result. It will be remembered, however, that in this portion of the state, which has been the

---

admission to the Union." Claude Elliott, "Union Sentiment in Texas, 1861-1865," *Southwestern Historical Quarterly,* L, 449; J. Lee and Lillian J. Stambaugh, *A History of Collin County, Texas* (Austin, 1958), 62.

As noted, the convention at Austin did submit the secession ordinance to a vote of the people of Texas. The "proposition" referred to by Diamond was outlined subsequently with specific demarcation of proposed boundaries ("meets and bounds").

[7]E. Junius Foster, editor of the Sherman *Patriot,* was shot and killed in October, 1862, at the doorstep of his print shop in Sherman, following publication in his newspaper of comments approving the assassination of Colonel William C. Young, a principal in the organization of the "Citizens Court" in Gainesville. A number of years later the colonel's son, James D. Young, made confession in court that he shot Foster after the editor's refusal to retract comment on the elder Young's death. Landrum, *Grayson County, An Illustrated History of Grayson County, Texas,* 65.

theatre of violence and general civil disturbances, the vote on the ordinance of Secession was largely in favor of the Union.[8]

There were men at the head of this scheme, bold intelligent and ambitious; but the adventure, like that of Aaron Burr, failing in its incipiency, it will probably never be known who matured the plan, nor what was the full scope and extent of the original design.

The operations of Burr on Blennerhassett Island, though insignificent in themselves and carried forward by only a handful of adventurers, were, however, the result of a magnificent plan, recognized by the Government in which he had held the highest office but one as the stepping stone to Empire.

The evidence elicited on the trial of Burr in the U. S. Supreme Court, for treason, discloses simply an intention on the part of Burr to revolutionize the sentiment of the people of the West, win them from their allegiance and establish and organize a separate government of which he should be the acknowledged head. Parties to a similar undertaking in Texas did not even receive public denunciation, but were allowed to assert and promulgate their treasonable doctrines with the greatest impunity. This bold dash in defiance of the Constitution and laws of the state gave the enemies of peace and good government in this section fresh courage, and with this moral weight in their favor, their operations were pushed forward with renewed energies.

The prospects of the "Order" were evidently in the ascendent until the final adoption of the Ordinance of Secession. This seemed to strike a fatal blow at the very root of their enterprise. The almost unparalleled unanimity of the people of the State in favor of disunion, and the enthusiasm manifested throughout the country in view of the establishment of a Southern Confederacy, caused a general panic and disquietude among them. Many of the Union men began to remove northward, and finally, under the proclamation of President Davis extending to such

[8] The statewide vote, based on returns reported by 122 counties, was 46,129 for secession; 14,697 against. Nineteen of these counties reported majority votes against withdrawing from the Union, eight of which were in North Texas: Collin, 948 against, 405 for; Cooke, 221 against, 137 for; Fannin, 656 against, 471 for; Grayson, 901 against, 463 for; Jack, 76 against, 14 for; Lamar, 663 against, 553 for; Montague, 86 against, 50 for; Wise, 78 against, 76 for. Winkler, *Journal of the Secession Convention of Texas, 1861*, p. 88.

the privilege of removing beyond the limits of the Confederacy, a great number returned to the United States.

Deprived of this great moral support, the members of the "Order" thought best to defer active operations, and those who remained were silent and passive, submissive to the rules of order and obedient to the mandates of the law.

But when war, relentless war, called the gallant sons of Texas from their happy homes and firesides and confined them to the tented field, the worst [fears] of those who watched the movements of the domestic enemy began to be realized. Many of the members went into the army, apparently in good faith; but afterwards, it was ascertained, they designed only to obtain an opportunity to confer with the Northern army upon subjects connected with their organization. And through the active agency of those hanging on the flanks and rear of the invading forces in Missouri, many of whom were well acquainted with this country and the members of the band, those who remained at home were kept constantly advised as to the progress of the "Order."

Looking with ardent hope for a strong force to reach Texas from Fort Scott through the Indian Territories, they at once began a vigorous prosecution of their favorite enterprise. They then began to contemplate the successful issue of their cherished design to subvert the state government, murder the innocent and unoffending women and children of Southern men, and destroy all property both public and private which could not be used to advantage in their scheme of rapine and plunder.

THE TIME OF ORGANIZATION

It has not been definitely ascertained at what exact time this wicked combination was dignified by the name of "Order," "Organization," or "Institution," as many of their leading members termed their association.

From the best information derived from various sources, they must have assumed their corporate existence and perfected their ritual at some period early in the spring of 1862. I. W. P. Lock,[9] under the limb, stated that he originated the "Order" himself; but the confessions of others clearly contradict this statement. It is quite probable that Capt. Lock had full authority to swear in and receive membership in his own immediate department, very much in his own way; but the volume of evidence shows the existence of the "Order" before Lock was in any manner connected with it. It is pretty clearly settled that they began operations under their "charter" early in 1862.

[9]I. W. P. Lock was one of the prisoners condemned by the "Citizens Court" and subsequently hanged. As will be seen in the text, he testified that he and Jackson Mounts "were the first starters of this order."

THE EXTENT OF THE ORDER

Before introducing any of the particulars connected with the progress of the "Order," it may be proper to inform the reader of the extent of its operations, and the scope of its designs.

None except those who are intimately acquainted with the particular incidents connected with it, the character of those engaged, and the localities selected for the field of their operations could ever possibly appreciate its magnitude.

The poor deluded wretches in Texas who fell victims to their own egregious folly were but tools in the hands of a more powerful wing of the same "Institution." They were but pioneers in the work, and to the premature & over-zealous efforts of a few to accomplish a purpose requiring the cooperation of all their forces, may be attributed their sad and untimely fate.

With the largest number that they ever claimed as belonging to the organization in Texas, they could not have hoped for success by their own efforts alone; and hence, it has ever been a source of profound wonder to those who are not acquainted and advised of the facts. The reader at the outset is astonished that so few should attempt such a hazardous work—that so few should contemplate the overthrow of a State government and murder indiscriminately its unoffending citizens; that so few should band themselves together in the face of a people already in arms, acquainted with war; and renowned for their prowess and military achievements.

But this astonishment yields when the mists of error are dispelled by the light of truth. It was ascertained beyond question that this insignificant band was in full fellowship with a like combination in the Federal army of the West, and linked with every hostile tribe of Indians then in arms against the South, and especially against Texas.

It is useless to attempt to vindicate their extraordinary conduct upon any other hypothesis than a direct assurance of timely aid from other sources. Strange as their conduct may seem, stranger things have occurred in our own country, and for the accomplishment of similar purposes.

Who, with a properly [*sic*] and well-balanced mind, endowed with reason and intelligence could have been induced to believe that old John Brown, the martyr, with but a squad of followers would have marched into the very heart of the Old Dominion, in time of peace and public tranquility, with fire and sword, slaying, burning and destroying whatever fell in his path? . . . [The writer here goes into an extensive discussion of John Brown's capture of Harper's Ferry, concluding:] Nobly did the Old Dominion meet the danger and vindicate the majesty of her laws and the liberty of her people by a practical application of her motto, "Sic Semper Tyrrannis."

So, in this instance in Texas, the promised and anticipated relief was not forthcoming in the hour of peril, and hence those who meditated the ruin and destruction of the fairest portion of this great state fell victims to their own criminal folly.

This organization was in league also with the nine tribes of Reserve Indians, except the Tonkawas; to wit, the Keechi's, Ioni's, Waco's, Wichita's, Caddo's, Towokona's, Anodarco's, and Comanche: The organization was also in communication with the hostile tribes of Shawnee's, Delaware's, and Kickapoos; and, also, the disaffected portion of the Cherokee's, Creeks, Seminole's and other tribes. It was not originally understood by the members of the order that they were to cooperate with the Indians. The "Institution" was more intimately connected with the northern Army, in which they claimed many members, principally those who had fled and escaped public justice in Texas.

The fact [is] that such an organization existed and it's designs were, by duly appointed messengers, properly laid before military commandants in the Federal Army, and their cooperation secured In reply to the assurances made by these couriers, that Texas was vulnerable and utterly defenseless, the Federal Officers, very naturally engaged to assist them. But, aid from this source coming too slow, and finally becoming doubtful, whether it [would] come at all, the organization turned its attention to the Indians and opened correspondence with them.

After some time had elapsed in perfecting thier[10] plans, operation began about the middle of August 1862. The hostile Indian tribe(s) begun [*sic*] to make demonstration upon Fort Cobb, which caused the Chickasaw Battalion stationed there to retire to Fort Arbuckle, and a general rush of citizens back into the interior. In consequence of this formidable attack, it was naturally and reasonably expected that the militia of the border counties would be called out to drive back the savage, which was accordingly, and very promptly, done by Brig. Genl. Wm. Hudson.[11] Thus the traitors saw their plans working admirably.

It was understood among them that they should all respond to the call, apparently in good faith; and when the militia were ordered far beyond the limits of Texas, those who were necessarily in the ranks, upon a given signal and signs from the enemy, should band together and turn their weapons upon their neighbors; while as many as possible were to remain at home [to] take advantage of the helpless condition of the country and murder, pillage and destroy; and if, finally, unable to hold the country, they were to join their friends in the enemy's camp.

But, luckily, the demonstration of the Savage being timid and undecided in its character—and considering the distance, the scarcity of provisions and forage, and the uncertainty of a successful pursuit—Genl. Hudson countermanded the order and the expedition was abandoned.

This circumstance alone, checked an outbreak at that time.

Thus chagrined, and cheated of their spoil, the members of the order became bolder and more defiant than before. They openly denounced the Government, and vowed organized resistance to the

---

10A consistent idiosyncrasy in Diamond's manuscript is the misspelling of the possessive pronoun "their." All subsequent instances have been corrected.

11William Hudson was born in South Carolina in about 1820 and settled in Cooke County in the 1850's after living for several years in Missouri. He and his wife Mary Jane are listed as family no. 10 in the 1860 census of Cooke County, in which he is described as a "Land Locater." When the Texas legislature in December, 1861, passed a general act to put the state upon a war footing, he was appointed a brigadier general in command of one of the thirty-six brigade districts created by the act. He was placed in command of District 1, which included Cooke, Montague, Jack, and fourteen other northwestern counties, with headquarters in Gainesville. Clifford D. Cates, *Pioneer History* of *Wise County* (Decatur, 1907), 117. On disclosure of the "Peace Party Conspiracy" in late September, 1862, he declared martial law in the district and issued orders requiring every able-bodied man not already in the military service to report for duty. Elliott, "Union Sentiment in Texas, 1861-1865," *Southwestern Historical Quarterly,* L, 451.

Conscript Law.[12] They became a terror to their southern neighbors, mechanics among them refused to work for southern men, while their whole conduct evinced a spirit of hate and revenge too intolerable to be borne. They now conceived the bold design of striking the blow themselves, at all hazards.

A large quantity of powder and other ordnance stores being deposited at Sherman and Gainsville[13] their first step was to obtain possession of it. This accomplished, they, [de]signed to hold the country, take possession of all the property or fight their way to the Federal Army. So perfect and systematic were their plans that they had parcelled out the property of Southern men among each other, and had decided upon the unfortunate young women who were marriageable and handsome, who should be spared for wives; the rest to be put to death, together with the children.

Some, under sentence, were asked, why so foul a purpose? Why murder the helpless women, and innocent little children? They answered that the women might interfere with them in the enjoyment of their new estates; and if order should ever be restored, [they] might dispossess them entirely. As for the children—as nits, if not destroyed, would turn to lice, so the offspring of bad men must follow in the footprints of their sires.

Other objects which might have been contemplated by them are not sufficiently developed by the evidence to warrant a notice of them here. If they had succeeded in this, other plans of still greater magnitude might have been built upon it. But, as their success could only have been commensurate with the success of northern arms in this quarter, it is not probable that they would ever have added another degree to their ritual, or another oath, to bind the consciences of men.

It is thought by many, however, that the scheme comprehended, as its ultimatum, the organization of a free state embracing northwestern Texas and the Chickasaw and Choctaw Nations—thus annihilating the only Indian tribes faithful and true to the South.

---

[12]The Confederate Congress passed its initial conscript law affecting able-bodied men 18 through 35 years of age on April 16, 1862. Alan C. Ashcraft, *Texas in the Civil War: a Résumé History* (Austin, 1962), 14.

[13]The word "Gainesville" was misspelled by Diamond throughout his manuscript. All subsequent instances have been corrected.

COUNTERACTING MOVEMENTS

About the first of September, 1862, the first steps were taken to ferret out the designs of the domestic enemy and devise measures of protective defense. It was only a short time previous to this that the people had ascertained that these restless men had really organized for their destruction and that they were bound together by the most solemn oaths to execute their wicked purposes.

This fact was ascertained beyond doubt from a gentleman who had received propositions to go into the order, accompanied with promises of a rich reward in the way of plunder and exemption from all liability to aid and support the cause of the South.

Accordingly, Genl. Wm. Hudson, Col. James Bourland,[14] Col. James J. Diamond,[15] Capt. Wm. C. Twitty,[16] Capt. C. L. Roff[17]

---

[14]James G. Bourland, born in South Carolina in 1803, settled in the Red River Valley in Texas during the Republic of Texas. He was appointed collector of customs for the Red River District in 1842. On the outbreak of the Mexican War he helped William C. Young raise a regiment of 1,000 volunteers in the Red River area. Bourland was appointed its lieutenant colonel. He served as a state senator in the First and Second Legislatures of the State of Texas. In 1856 he was conducting a general store in Bourland's Bend of the Red River in Cooke County in partnership with Austin Brooks. The 1860 census of Cooke County lists him as a fifty-seven-year-old farmer.

Upon the secession of Texas Bourland returned to military service and subsequently commanded a regiment organized for the protection of the northern frontier of Texas against marauding Indians and federal guerrillas. Units of his regiment were stationed on the Red River, principally at Preston in Grayson County and at old Warren in Fannin County. He died in 1868. Mattie Davis Lucas and Mita Holsapple Hall, *A History of Grayson County, Texas* (Sherman, 1936), 87, 128; *Biographical Souvenir of the State of Texas* (Chicago, 1889), 98.

[15]James J. Diamond was the eldest of six brothers who moved to Texas from their native county of De Kalb, Georgia, before the Civil War. He settled in Grayson County near present-day Whitesboro. A cotton planter and slave owner in the Red River valley portion of northwestern Grayson County, he was the leading spokesman in that area for Southern rights and views in the days immediately preceding the Civil War. He attended the 1860 Democratic National Convention at Charleston, South Carolina, as a delegate from Texas and bolted as a member of that delegation upon the nomination of Douglas for president.

Upon the election of Lincoln in November, 1860, James J. Diamond was instrumental in calling a public meeting of Grayson and Cooke county citizens at Whitesboro on November 23, 1860, "to take into consideration the present political condition of the country." His brother John R. Diamond was called upon to preside. James J. Diamond, as chairman of a committee of fifteen named by the meeting, offered a resolution calling upon Governor Sam Houston "to ascertain the will of

and others met in the town of Gainesville, Cooke County, for the purpose of maturing some plan by which they might obtain the secret schemes and operations of the conspirators.

After a long consultation, they agreed to appoint, or designate, some suitable person to make application and receive a regular initiation into the order, obtain the signs, grip & password and all information necessary to a full understanding of the character of that class of citizens with whom they had to deal, as well as the names of those of which the "Order" was composed.

In the first instance, they very properly selected J. B. McCurley to whom propositions had been made to join the organization. Mr. McCurley,[18] a good citizen and a gentleman of fine intelligence, proceeded at once, under full instructions to the discharge of the duty assigned him. He made application, and was duly re-

---

the people ... by convention, or otherwise" on the question of Texas remaining in the Union. He also moved that a company of 100 men be organized at once in the two counties to help defend "Southern interest and Southern equality in the Union, or out of it." Both resolutions carried with only four votes against them.

James J. Diamond attended the Secession Convention in Austin as one of Cooke County's two delegates. He was named a member of the Convention's Committee of Public Safety, which in effect took revolutionary control of the state in the interim between the recess of the convention on February 4, 1861, and its re-assembly on March 2 to announce the ratification at the polls of the ordinance of secession. He was named lieutenant colonel of the 11th Texas Cavalry upon its organization in the spring of 1861, participating in its occupation of the Indian Territory. He succeeded to its colonelcy upon the death of Colonel William C. Young in October, 1862. He died in Houston, Texas, during the yellow fever epidemic of 1867. Lucas and Hall, *A History of Grayson County, Texas,* 125.

[16]William C. Twitty was born in Kentucky in 1801 and lived for a number of years in Louisiana before moving to Texas in the fall of 1836. While in Louisiana he married Elizabeth Montague, daughter of Daniel Montague. Twitty was among the first settlers in Cooke County west of Gainesville. He died a few years after the end of the Civil War, and his widow made her home at Marysville, Cooke County. A. Morton Smith, *First 100 Years in Cooke County* (San Antonio, 1955), 20.

[17]In October, 1862, Charles L. Roff was captain of a cavalry company in Brigadier General William Hudson's brigade of state troops, and later served as major of Bourland's Cavalry Regiment. C. N. Jones, *Early Days in Cooke County* (Gainesville, 1936), 67.

[18]J. B. McCurley, from Tennessee, was a forty-eight-year-old farmer in Denton County in 1860. He and his family had come to Texas in the 1850's by way of Illinois. U. S. Eighth Census, 1860 (Returns of Schedule 1, Free Inhabitants, for Denton County, Texas, microfilm, Dallas Public Library). In Diamond's opinion, as given in his "Review of McCurley," this carrier of the mail between Gainesville and Denton provided the initial clue in the discovery of the "Peace Party Conspiracy." Previously published accounts have credited Newton J. Chance with having first discovered the existence of the Unionist resistance group in Cooke County. Elliott, "Union Sentiment in Texas, 1861-1865," *Southwestern Historical Quarterly,* L, 449.

ceived and admitted into the order and made acquainted with all the secrts [*sic*] & mysteries connected with it.

How he proceeded in the part assigned him may be better and more fully explained by his testimony given [before] the "Citizens Court" on the trial of Dr. Henry Childs.[19] And it may be proper to remark here that nowhere in the proceedings of the Court has any testimony been incorporated in this report, (except the voluntary confessions of the parties condemned) unless it has been sanctioned by an oath, administered under the forms of law by officers authorized to administer oaths and elicited according to the rules of evidence.

19Henry Childs was the central figure in the "Peace Party Conspiracy," in view of the author of this narrative. His opinion also reflects the views and convictions of members of the "Citizens Court." Diamond himself was not a participant in the events he chronicles or a resident of Cooke County at the time of the Great Hanging at Gainesville, although, as explained in his "Introduction," he arrived at the scene shortly afterward. The absence of the name of Henry Childs in available contemporary records of Cooke County, including the federal census of 1860, may be explained by Diamond's statement that Childs "came from Missouri to Texas but a few years anterior to the war between the States."

McCURLEY'S TESTIMONY

I met Ephraim Childs[20] at the Hotel in the town of Gainesville, sometime in the month of September 1862. After some conversation he remarked to me, "Would you like to go into a Society for the good of our country?" He then, before any remarked [*sic*] made by me, continued—"You are a good union man, are you not?" I told him I had been one. He then said, "Come into the room, it may be that you are one still."

We went into the room, and he gave me some signs, which I did not understand and of course, could not answer them. He then remarked, "You know nothing about it." We then walked out on the porch, when he said further: "If you want to know all about it, my brother, the Doctor, is one of the head men and he will initiate you."

I told him perhaps at some future time, I would stop and endeavor to learn something for the good of the country, for, I thought it in a condition to need all the aid that could be extended to it, and that I was anxious to do all the good in my power. He then said, "These d——d rebel rascals about town (and there are a good many of them) have a large quantity of ammuni[tion] and we Union men intend to have it, and that d——d soon."

I made no reply and left him. I informed Col. Bourland of what I had heard and he advised me to go on, join the order and get all the information I could on the subject.

About two weeks subsequent to the time of the interview with Childs I came to Gainesville, and Col. Bourland loaned me a horse and I rode out to the residence of Doctor Henry Childs, finding him at home. I inquired about some estray stock which (as I told him) I learned run in his neighborhood. After some conversation, I told him I had formed an acquaintance with his brother in Gainesville, and that he had informed me of the existence of an organization in the country, which he styled the Union party, and that being myself a Union man, the idea pleased me very much. I then stated to him that his brother told me that he (the Doctor) could give me all information and full instructions regarding said organization. This seemed to please him, and without any further remarks on my part he replied, "I must first swear you to secrecy."

At his bidding I then raised my hand and took the following obligation: "You, J. B. McCurley, in the presence of Almighty God, do most solemnly promise and swear that you will forever keep secret

[20]Ephraim Childs, the brother of Dr. Henry Childs, was credited with unwittingly first having revealed the existence of the secret order.

the revelations now about to be made to you, and that you will obey all the orders of the society into which you are now about to be initiated. So help you, God."

I then told him that his brother had informed me of an intention on the part of the Society to rise very soon and capture all the ammunition deposited in town, and that I desired to know when the seizure was to take place. He replied, "there is a talk about it," but he thought they would delay it awhile longer. I then asked him how many his Order numbered. He said they not only numbered hundreds, but they were counted by the thousands—that their Institution reached from the north to the South, through the northern and Southern armies, and that within the last eight days he had sworn in and initiated over fifty members.

I asked him if he had taken their names. He replied, "No; but we know each other by the signs." He then drew from his pocket a small blank book and showed me that they used dots, or characters other than words, as he said, to avoid detection.

He then read from the book the obligations which bound them to protect and defend each other at all times and under all circumstances, even unto death. He said they would not probably take up arms against the State until the Northern army should come in, when they were to rise and fight against the Secessionists, or fall in the rear of the Federal army. He said that a new governor would soon be inaugurated and take his seat in Austin—that Jim Lane[21] of Kansas was talked of for the place, but that he thought Sam Houston would be selected, as the most available man & popular with all parties.

I then inquired of him from what quarter the Northern army was to come into Texas. He said from above this place, or from Kansas and Galveston, the two divisions of the army to meet at Austin—that there was a regular correspondence kept up between the Order and the Federal army, the latter being well and fully posted as to the strength and objects of their organization and the weakness of the rebels, and that through the energy and influence of the Society, the Northern army & our friends were informed that they might now enter Texas in perfect safety.

Having spoken of "our friends," I asked him who were our friends? He answered, "the Union men." I asked who were our enemies. He answered the Southern secessionists. Having in the conversation used the word "tories," I asked him who he called tories. He replied, the secession party [of the] South. I asked him what would become of them, in the event of the success of the order and the occupation of

---

[21]James Henry Lane (1814-1866) resigned from the United States Senate as a Senator from the State of Kansas in 1861 to command a brigade of volunteers as a brigadier general. Born in Indiana, he served as lieutenant governor of that state and then as a representative in Congress before emigrating to the Territory of Kansas in 1855. He was a close friend of Abraham Lincoln and an organizer of the Republican Party.

the country by the Northern army. He said in reply that "when our friends come in, if they should not submit, the last one of them would be killed."

He then informed me that he could give me signs, words and grips by which I might know any member of the order, if I would consent to be sworn again. He said he desired to swear me, and give me power to swear in others, I declined for the want of time then, but told him I would call again soon, and learn all about the organization.

REVIEW OF McCURLEY

In reviewing the testimony of this man McCurley, many remarkable features in the design and operations of the order are prominent and quite noticeable. While McCurley was nothing but an implement in the hands of others to detect and expose the inside workings of the "Order," he was nevertheless a man that stood fair among his neighbors and whose evidence was received as the truth, and not questioned or denied by the accused or his friends.

He was a man of ripe age & at that time was engaged in carrying the mail between Denton and Gainesville. He was known to be fond of a social glass with his friends at times, but ever on the alert and quite sound in his suspicions of those with whom he had intercourse.

Had it not been for the exceeding volubility of the younger Childs (Ephraim) superinduced by an overflow, or overdose, of bad Confederate whiskey, he would not in all probability have led the sagacious McCurley to suspect the worst from the organization in which he boasted of being an active member. And but for these voluntary communications, he might have lived to be useful in his favorite "Institution," and witnessed its triumph in crime and wickedness.

Being intoxicated, he felt equal to any emergency and forgot for the time being the oath of secrecy and the necessity of that caution so necessary to carry out purposes for which they were organized. His object was to gain the sympathies of McCurley by referring to his record as a Union man. McCurley discloses no disposition to learn or go into any thing further than to frankly admit that he would be pleased with the restoration of the Union upon any fair or honorable means. But when he was informed that this was to be accomplished by means of signs, grips and passwords, and the murder of his neighbors and the betrayal of his section into the hands of an unscrupulous, heterogeneous, reckless organization, he seems to shudder at the idea and declined to receive any further information.

At his first interview with Childs, not withstanding he pressed the matter with such earnestness, McCurley's conduct shows that he did not clearly see any "good to the country" in the movement suggested for his endorsement and cooperation. He could see no "good to his country" in attacking and sacking the town with fire and sword, and the killing of neighbors, the "rebel rascals" designated as objects of revenge. Therefore, he "made no reply and left him."

After introducing himself to Dr. Henry Childs at the suggestion of citizens heretofore mentioned, McCurley discovered that the oath taken before him led him on one step further into the secrets of the order. He was to "obey all orders of the Society." He then seems inclined to [have] avoid[ed] any further oath-taking, and introduced a system of inquiry based upon the information already obtained in a manner worthy of the most erudite and cunning barrister. It was at least creditable to a plain and unpretending countryman.

The strength of the order rapidly spreading was put down by Childs at thousands, which he probably thought sufficient to guarantee any member against capture or punishment. When asked the names of those in this section belonging to the society, Childs very properly declined to give them, fearing no doubt that McCurley would recognize the names of many with whom he would scorn to associate with as "Union men." This dodge doubtless seduced many into this order who, at the first blush, would not have consented to have attached themselves to the organization if all the plans had been submitted and explained to them. That "Union Men" were thus approached who emphatically declined [to join] cannot be denied; but it seems that when once in, they accorded their active assistance and full fellowship with the "Order" in the vilest and darkest transactions.

But [the joiner] had still another step to take—"to protect and defend each other to the death."

The suggestion that Jim Lane of Kansas, or Sam Houston of Texas would be inaugurated in Austin at an early day was a piece of deception palpably as transparent as it was ungenerous and unjust to the name and now the memory of the great, and distinguished lamented General Sam Houston.

The association of these two names together, the one infamous and the other illustrious, was done for a two-fold purpose: First, to induce the applicant to believe that Jim Lane, then in Command of the Federal troops in Kansas & West Missouri, was actually making preparations for a movement against Texas (which was probably really the case) and that, in the event of such a movement, the order and its members were sure of success.

Secondly, if the great Houston should stand at the head of a general movement to resist the organized state and Confederate Governments, that his powerful name and universal popularity, connected with the military operations of his associate, Jim Lane, would assure the success of the scheme beyond peradventure. The representation that this would be consummated by the Federal armies approaching from the north and by way of Galveston, and a final juncture at Austin, was not without reasonable plausibility, and it is well known that military operations at that time really indicated such a purpose.

The announcement by Childs that when the Federal Army should come in, all who did not quietly submit would be killed, appears to have staggered McCurley for the second time in the progress of his work, and pleading want of time to go any further, left the Doctor to ponder over the events of the approaching revolution, as they should transpire; and instead of receiving the signs, grips and passwords which were offered him he hastened from his presence to join a committee of friends to relate what he had heard.

FURTHER PROGRESS OF THE CITIZENS

These statements of a man in whom all confidence could possibly be placed caused the gentlemen before referred to, to doubt no longer the full scope and designs of the "Order." But still unwilling to hazard a general disturbance of the apparent tranquility, and apprehensive of doing injustice and violence to any innocent persons, the committee thought proper to make further inquiries and ascertain if possible the full details, and the names of the members of the organization. It was resolved, therefore, to select Col. N. J. Chance,[22] a man full of bone and muscle, courage and intelligence who, under the instructions of the committee, made the necessary application, joined the Society and obtained in detail its inside workings.

---

[22]Newton J. Chance, a resident of Wise County, was stationed in Gainesville as a member of Brigadier General William Hudson's command at the time the existence of the secret order was first reported to military authorities. Smith, *First 100 Years in Cooke County*, 35; Elliott, "Union Sentiment in Texas, 1861-1865," *Southwestern Historical Quarterly*, L, 451; Cates, *Pioneer History of Wise County*, 131.

Some quarter of a century after the Great Hanging at Gainesville, Chance was apprehended and tried at Sherman for the murder of E. Junius Foster, editor of the Sherman *Patriot*, in October, 1862. Chance subsequently had become a minister in the Christian Church. He was acquitted following the surprise confession in the trial by James D. Young that it was he, not Chance, who had fired the fatal shotgun blast that ended the life of the editor. Landrum, *Grayson County, An Illustrated History of Grayson County, Texas*, 65.

COL. N. J. CHANCE'S TESTIMONY

Immediately after being appointed to this delicate and responsible trust, Col. Chance visited the residence of Dr. Henry Childs and was regularly initiated, took all the degrees & received the signs, grip, and passwords, and was duly commissioned to swear in others. When he had obtained the secrets of the "Institution" and had learned a great many of the names of its members, he reported to the Committee.

As the testimony of Col. Chance will appear in the proceedings on the trial of Dr. Henry Childs, it is not deemed necessary to introduce it here. His evidence strictly corroborates that given by McCurley, fully confirms the Committee in their apprehensions of an immediate outbreak. The organization had so far attained its ends, that nothing was lacking but a fit opportunity to make known its designs only in their execution. While this committee was by day and by night earnestly engaged in the prosecution of a well-planned project to defeat the Conspirators and save bloodshed, the people generally were very prudently kept from a knowledge of its operations; in fact, no one knew anything concerning the existence of such a committee except the very few employed to aid and further its progress.

Accordingly, there being no further time to lose, the following named citizens met together to consider how to avoid the impending danger—to wit: Col. James Bourland, Col. Daniel Montague,[23]

---

[23]Diamond's narrative throws additional light on the life of Daniel Montague, one of the most important leaders in North Texas during the Republic of Texas and in the early years of Texas' statehood. Montague County was named for him upon its creation in 1858.

Montague was born on August 22, 1798, in South Hadley, Massachusetts. He moved to Louisiana in 1820 and was a surveyor there during the next fifteen years. He set out to aid the Texas revolutionists in their struggle against Mexico in 1836 but arrived too late to take part in the Battle of San Jacinto. Returning to Louisiana to gather his family around him, he moved to the Republic of Texas later that same year, settling first at old Warren on the Red River in present Fannin County. He conducted a general merchandise store in partnership with William Henderson, then accepted the post of surveyor of the Fannin Land District that included much of present Cooke, Grayson, and other North Texas counties. He was a noted Indian fighter. Upon the outbreak of the Mexican War he helped raise a regiment of Red River volunteers and commanded a company as captain.

Daniel Montague moved westward along the Red River in the late 1840's, taking

Col. N. J. Chance, Col. W. C. Twitty, Major C. L. Roff, William Peery,[24] J. M. Peery,[25] J. C. Chance, Samuel C. Doss and others. How well they laid and executed their plan of operations, the subsequent pages of this work are designed fully to show. They resolved to meet the danger at once and to meet it boldly. They selected from the good people of the county a sufficient number of men, in the vicinity of each member of the order, to seize upon the person named at a certain hour on a certain day. These true and good men having received their orders through the proper medium and the time fixed for their execution, the critical moment had at last arrived.

---

up land in Cooke County, of which he became county surveyor. He also had surveyed much of the area that became Montague County. The 1850 census of Cooke County, Texas, lists him as 52 years of age, engaged in farming, and possessed of land valued at $5,000.

Montague's principal service to the Confederacy, as this narrative discloses, was as president of the "Citizens Court" that tried, condemned, and hanged the thirty-nine prisoners charged with disloyalty and treason to the State of Texas. Montague is also shown as foreman of the grand jury which in November, 1862, returned an indictment against Joel Francis De Lemeron on a charge of treason. The case was tried in the fall term of 1862 before the district court at Gainesville.

Montague was among the ex-Confederates who refused to accept the outcome of the War Between the States and emigrated to Mexico in 1865. He lived for the next eleven years in the valley of the Tuxpan River. He returned to Texas in 1876 to make his home with his widowed daughter, Elizabeth Montague Twitty, at Marysville, Cooke County, where he died on December 20 of that year. His return to Texas and subsequent death are significant in establishing the probable date of Diamond's final draft of his narrative, as is obvious from the text of his manuscript. Lucas and Hall, *A History of Grayson County, Texas,* 40-41; Z. T. Fulmore, *History and Geography of Texas as Told in County Names* (Austin, 1915), 86-87.

[24]William Peery, a native of Kentucky, was enumerated as a sixty-year-old farmer living in Cooke County, in the 1860 federal census. He had lived for a time in Missouri before moving to Texas with his wife and three children in 1851. U. S. Eighth Census, 1860 (Returns of Schedule 1, Free Inhabitants, for Cooke County, Texas, microfilm, Dallas Public Library), family no. 551.

[25]Presumably a brother of William Peery, James M. Peery was a member of the Masonic Lodge at Gainesville in 1859. He served as a member of the patrol at Gainesville as provided by state law in 1861. Smith, *First 100 Years in Cooke County,* 39.

THE ARREST

Accordingly, precisely at daylight on the morning of the first of October, 1862, every one so far as known (except those who had escaped) were seized and placed in custody, "in the name and by the authority of the people of the County of Cooke, State of Texas."

Large quantities of ammunition and fire arms were captured in the possession and upon the persons of the accused.

DOC EDMONSON

Many escaped through the treachery of one Doc Edmonson. Being a son-in-law of one of the oldest and best citizens then residing on the western line of Grayson County, and who was himself a native of Illinois, he was informed of the contemplated arrest by those whom he had induced to regard him as a friend. As soon as he could shun his friends, he mounted his horse and notified many of the members of their danger. So zealous was he in the execution of trust and faithful in observing his oath he forgot to be merciful to his beast; for it is well known that the poor animal was so violently urged on his mission that he died early the next day. Edmonson fled but at the close of the war came back to the country. After enjoying the friendship and hospitality of his old friends and neighbors for several years, [he] returned to Kansas.

Some, however, who had the advantage of Edmonson's warning refused to take his advice, and after the first arrest gave themselves up voluntarily, believing the "Order" strong enough to release them.

HEAVY RAIN FALL

At the very hour when the arrests were made all over the county a perfect deluge of rain was falling, and the heavens darkened with a raging storm cloud. But the guards were true to their trusts and, not withstanding the drenching rain, they never faltered in the discharge of their duty.

Large quantities of powder, lead and cartridges were found concealed in beds, ladies' wearing apparel & in every conceivable secret place. *The weeping wives* of the accused evinced great alarm and the deepest concern for the safety of their husbands from the beginning. They owned to entertain strange presentments that their husbands could not escape punishment while some of them seemed to be well instructed concerning the organization, and failed to appreciate the danger or properly consider the punishment due such transgressions.

The most intense excitement now prevailed throughout the county. There was a general motion of guards, prisoners, citizens, screaming women and children, from every section toward Gainesville—a rush of those who escaped to places of rendezvous to organize for the rescue, while the citizens grasped their guns and organized for defense. All were active and fully alive to a sense of the danger & peril of the next act in the exciting drama.

If there was one class of participants in that rushing throng, in that Babel of excitement and domestic disorder, that was more calm and impurterbed [*sic*] than another, it was that composed of the prisoners. They, between sixty and seventy in number, were marched by many different roads into the town of Gainesville, lodged in a strong prison home and orders for their safe detention rigidly enforced. But they seemed confident of the power of their friends to release them, saying there were enough members of the "Order" to rescue them upon a given signal. So implicitly did they rely upon the courage and strength of their brotherhood that they defiantly informed the guards and people that they were not at all alarmed and only went into prison as a matter of choice —to give their friends a better opportunity to release them without danger to themselves.

They were encouraged in this belief by a circumstance that occurred in Gainesville in the preceeding [*sic*] month of July. At that time a charge was preferred against one of their number, (as was afterwards ascertained) who was arrested by Col. James Bourland, Provost Marshal. After proper investigation, the accused was discharged. It was observed while his trial was pending that an unusual assemblage gathered around the marshal's office, unwarranted by any ostensible object, there being no cause for public excitement at that period. It was also a mysterious and noticeable fact that nearly all who assembled on that occasion "happened to bring their guns along."

And when it was discovered that the prisoners were so confidently relying upon their friends to rescue them, the people could look back to the trial of Cottrell[26] before the Provost Marshal and connect them with the strange popular assemblage of that day. And by this circumstance the fact was plainly developed that if Cottrell had been ordered to prison, the Society was then ready and able to rescue him.

A dispatch had been sent to Fort Washita calling upon the Commander of that post for assistance. And other neighboring commands [were] promptly notified of the situation of affairs in Cooke County. These commands having readily responded to the call made upon them and the citizens having organized for safety and defense, the excitement and anxiety was measurably allayed.

The following commands soon reached Gainesville, in the order in which they are named: A militia company from Grayson County, commanded by Capt. Russell;[27] one company from Col. Charles DeMorse's[28] Regiment, CSA, commanded by Capt. [Nick]

26John Cottrell was one of two Cooke County soldiers in Captain James D. Young's company of Major J. S. Randolph's battalion, Partisan Rangers, who were subsequently arrested in connection with the "Peace Party Conspiracy." Insisting upon a court martial, they were convicted by such a court and hanged.

27Probably John Russell, since a John Russell served as a captain in the 11th Texas Cavalry and three John Russells are listed in the U. S. Eighth Census, 1860 (Returns of Schedule 1, Free Inhabitants, for Grayson County, Texas, microfilm, Dallas Public Library).

28Charles DeMorse was the founder and long-time editor of the *Northern Standard* at Clarksville. He took up arms in behalf of the Confederacy after strenuously opposing the secession of Texas and its adherence to the Confederate States of America. In 1862 he organized the 29th Texas Cavalry, of which he became colonel. He had been born in Leicester, Massachusetts, on January 31, 1816, and had come to Texas in the summer of 1836. He died at Clarksville in 1887. Ernest Wallace, *Charles DeMorse: Pioneer Editor and Statesman* (Lubbock, 1943).

Wilson; the entire militia of Denton County, commanded by Col. Patton;[29] two Companies from Fort Washita, C.N., under Capts. Marshall and Bumpass[30] and one company from Major Randolph's Battalion, CSA, under Capt. [James D.] Young. The prompt and meritorious conduct of Major Randolph in the premises, is fully explained in the following dispatch to Cols. Bourland and Young:

The dispatch reads:

Camp Tishomingo, October 4, 1862, Gentlemen.

I am informed that quite a number of men, belonging to this Battalion, are implicated by your investigation of the treasonable plot in Cooke County. If so, please give me a list of their names. All who are implicated here, are subject to your orders, and it will be my greatest pleasure to arrest them, and if necessary assist you in hanging them. If you need any more assistance, my services, and those of every true southern man here, are at your disposal. Please forward at once the names of every one who should be arrested. Respectfully, J. S. Randolph, Major. Comdg. Bat. Par Ran. CSA.

In the meantime, the militia of Cooke County had been organized under the able supervision of Brig. Genl. Wm. Hudson, and placed under the command of that gallant Col. W. C. Twitty. Sentinels were placed on every road approaching the town and the troops kept constantly in line of battle. Reliable information had been received that the members of the "Order" had organized and were preparing for an immediate attack upon the town under the leadership of the Rev. Capt. Garrison, a Northern minister, whose short residence in the country had inspired his neighbors with more fear of his villainies than respect for his Christianity.

On the night of October 2 1862, the citizens' picket encountered Capt. Garrison's force about eight miles from Gainesville, a few shots exchanged, when Capt. Garrison halted for the purpose of reconortering [*sic*]. At this juncture, one of the order deserted from town and informed Capt. Garrison of the strength of the citizens' forces. This caused his retreat into Red River bottom, where it is thought in a short time he disbanded his

---

29Probably S. P. C. Patton, who served as a captain in Bourland's Cavalry Regiment and is listed in the U. S. Eighth Census, 1860 (Returns of Schedule 1, Free Inhabitants, for Denton County, Texas, microfilm, Dallas Public Library).

30Probably A. B. or Abner M. Marshall and John K. Bumpass, captains in Martin's Partisan Ranger Battalion.

forces and left each man to provide for his own safety. This company numbered about eighty men. Lock, Harper[31] and other prominent leaders in different portions of the county having been arrested & imprisoned, their respective commands did not cooperate with Capt. Garrison in time to effect the release of the prisoners until the opposing strength became too formidable for any hope of success. Hence the abandonment of the attempt on the part of Garrison. Though for several days afterwards it was asserted by the prisoners and their friends that there still existed an organized, well-armed force strong enough to effect their escape and that they were sworn to do it, or die in the effort.

Pending these extraordinary proceedings an incident occurred which illustrates the great alarm felt, and the bold determination of the people to defend themselves and punish the guilty.

Before any assistance had arrived the sentinels reported the approach of an armed force from the West.[32] Not knowing whether it was friendly or hostile, Col. Twitty rode out to meet it. Galloping up in speaking distance, he addressed the officer in command as follows, "What command, sir?" "Capt. Russells Company," was the reply. "Where from?" demanded Col. T. "Grayson County." "Where are you going, sir?" "To Gainesville." "For what purpose?" "We have understood you needed help; and have come to aid you." "The people of Cooke County have not called upon the people of Grayson for help," [said Colonel Twitty] "therefore I would inquire by what authority you come." Capt. Russell then advanced and in a firm tone said, "We are Southern men, sir, citizens of Grayson Co., and have come in the name of the Southern people to aid the good citizens of Cooke County in their efforts to vindicate the laws and to uphold them in their right of self defense." "Welcome," replied Col. Twitty, and taking Capt. Russell by the hand thanked him for his sympathy and timely aid of himself and company.

---

[31]M. D. Harper was a thirty-three-year-old carpenter born in Virginia, who settled in Cooke County after 1850, according to the 1860 federal census. He was condemned and hanged by order of the "Citizens Court." U. S. Eighth Census, 1860 (Returns of Schedule 1, Free Inhabitants, for Cooke County, Texas, microfilm, Dallas Public Library).

[32]The author may have erred in stating the direction from which the armed force arrived from Grayson County, which lies to the east of Cooke County.

Simultaneously with the order of arrest, a county meeting was called, which was attended by almost the entire adult male population of the county. The meeting was held on the same day the arrests were made.

PUBLIC MEETING

In pursuance of a general notice a meeting of the citizens of Cooke County was held the 1st day of October 1862. The following proceedings were recorded to wit—On motion, Col. W. C. Young[33] was called to the chair, and J. M. Peery appointed secretary. Col. Young being requested to state the object of the meeting, arose and addressed the audience as follows:

FELLOW CITIZENS. The information having been received by the people of Cooke County that a vile and secret organization existed in their midst, having for its objects the overthrow of the government both State and Confederate, the seizure and destruction of property, both public and private; the perfecting of an alliance with the invading armies, both civilized and uncivilized now gathering upon our borders, and the indiscriminate slaughter of ourselves, our wives and children, it becomes our duty to adopt some plan to stay these impending evils, and marshal our strength in self defense.

---

[33]William Cocke Young was born in Davidson County, Tennessee, on May 12, 1812. He came to Texas during the days of the republic, settling first near Pecan Point in present Red River County in 1837. He was the first sheriff of Red River County and served as district attorney for the Seventh Judicial District by appointment of President Sam Houston.

Young was a member of General E. H. Tarrant's expedition that routed the last Indian settlement in the Dallas-Fort Worth area in 1841. He was a delegate to the convention at Austin in 1845 which accepted the terms of the annexation of Texas to the United States. During the Mexican War he raised and commanded a regiment of 1,000 Red River volunteers.

In 1851, Young moved to Grayson County, where he practiced law and occupied land formerly embraced in Shawneetown adjoining the present city of Denison. He served a term as United States Marshal. He moved from Grayson County to Cooke County in 1858, having established a new plantation home in the Sivil's Bend area of the Red River.

Upon the secession of Texas, Young was called by President Jefferson Davis to Montgomery, Alabama, first capital of the Confederacy, for consultations. On return to Texas he organized, in May, 1861, what was to become the 11th Texas Cavalry, composed of companies from Grayson, Cooke, Collin, Denton, and seven other north and northeast Texas counties.

Young was home in Cooke County on leave from his regiment because of poor health in the fall of 1862 and participated in moves to apprehend and punish members of the "Peace Party Conspiracy." It was from his river plantation that he went to rescue James Dixon only to meet his own death at the hands of unknown persons in the "brakes" of the Red River. Young County subsequently was named in his honor. Lucas and Hall, *A History of Grayson County, Texas*, 67; Landrum, *Grayson County, An Illustrated History of Grayson County, Texas*, 64; U. S. Eighth Census, 1860 (Returns of Schedule 1, Free Inhabitants, for Cooke County, Texas, microfilm, Dallas Public Library).

How wisely and well these plans were laid is now sufficiently developed in their successful execution. The result is, quite a number of those who cherished the wicked designs to accomplish our utter ruin have been arrested and confined in prison. The price of liberty is eternal vigilance, and I thank God that through the patriotic zeal, extreme caution and vigilance of the citizens of Cooke County, this infamous plot was discovered in time to save the country from the ruthless hand of the domestic traitor, robber and murder[er]. I understand the object of this meeting to be to advance by proper and legitimate means the work already begun. I am quite confident that you will all agree with me when I say that something *must be done* to check these conspirators in their villainous schemes and arrest the further progress of their wicked machinations. This is due to ourselves, to God and humanity.

As for me, while my whole heart is honestly earnestly enlisted for the defense of my common country, I regard it as my first duty to stand by my family fireside and not abandon my wife and children to the lawlessness and violence of my designing neighbors; and I am well assured from the number of good men of the County of Cooke assembled here today that the people are of the same mind. While I hope that wisdom & moderation may characterize our further proceedings, I still hope that no man will falter in this hour of trial. We have met to *act.* There is a *duty* for every one to perform. Something must be done; and trusting confidently to your wisdom and virtue, and having a common interest with mine, I ask you in the name of humanity what shall be done?

On motion, it was unanimously resolved that a committee of five good and true men, citizens of Cooke County, be appointed by the chairman, whose duty it should be to select twelve good true and lawful men citizens of the county to act as jurors, empowered to investigate, examine and decide upon all cases that should be brought before them.

Whereupon the chair appointed on said committee William Peery, Jas. B. Davenport,[34] R. G. Piper,[35] Aaron Hill[36] and J. B.

[34]James B. Davenport was born in Kentucky in 1801 and took up land for farming in Cooke County in the 1850's. He served as a member of the town patrol at Gainesville in 1861. Smith, *First 100 Years in Cooke County,* 32; U. S. Eighth Census, 1860 (Returns of Schedule 1, Free Inhabitants, for Cooke County, Texas, microfilm, Dallas Public Library).

[35]R. G. Piper, Chief Justice of Cooke County in 1862, was born in Virginia in 1815. He moved to Texas after 1850, taking up land for farming in Cooke County. *Ibid.*

[36]Aaron Hill was born in South Carolina in 1795. He moved to Texas with his family in 1848, receiving a patent in 1850 for 640 acres in Cooke County. He is listed in the 1850 Census, Grayson County, Texas, family no. 159, but moved,

Stone,[37] whose appointments were then unanimously endorsed by the meeting.

This com. retired and after consultation, recommended as the Jury of twelve the following names:[38] Samuel A. Doss, John W. Hamill,[39] Reason Jones,[40] Ben Scanland,[41] J. P. Long,[42] W. J. Simpson,[43] Wiley Jones,[44] Thomas Barrett,[45] Danl Montague, J. A.

---

apparently, to Cooke County the same year, being elected district clerk of Cooke County in 1850. Smith, *First 100 Years in Cooke County,* 31; Seymour V. Connor, *The Peters Colony of Texas* (Austin, 1959), 282; U. S. Seventh Census, 1850 (Returns of Schedule 1, Free Inhabitants, for Cooke County, Texas, microfilm, Dallas Public Library), family no. 159; U. S. Eighth Census, 1860 (Returns of Schedule 1, Free Inhabitants, for Cooke County, Texas, microfilm, Dallas Public Library).

37J. B. Stone was born in Virginia in 1823. He was a practicing physician in Gainesville at the time of the Great Hanging in 1862. *Ibid.*

38Reference to each of the twelve jurors is made below by the author under his heading of "Character of Court."

39John W. Hamill was one of the two ministers named to serve on the "Citizens Court."

40Reason Jones was born in Tennessee in 1813 and settled in Cooke County as a farmer in the 1850's. U. S. Eighth Census, 1860 (Returns of Schedule 1, Free Inhabitants, for Cooke County, Texas, microfilm, Dallas Public Library).

41Ben Scanland was born in Tennessee in 1818. He settled in Cooke County after 1850, taking up land to farm. He was named a member of the first grand jury empanelled in Cooke County (1858). *Ibid.;* Smith, *First 100 Years in Cooke County,* 25.

42J. Pope Long, a land owner in the Sivil's Bend area in Cooke County, was one of two physicians appointed on the "Citizens Court." He later moved to the Coesfield community of Cooke County. *Ibid.*

43W. J. Simpson was born in Tennessee in 1812. He moved to Texas after 1850, taking up land in Cooke County to farm. U. S. Eighth Census, 1860 (Returns of Schedule 1, Free Inhabitants, for Cooke County, Texas, microfilm, Dallas Public Library).

44Wiley Jones, a fifty-six-year-old farmer in 1860, was born in North Carolina. He was a member of the commissioners court of Cooke County in 1861. *Ibid.;* Smith, *First 100 Years in Cooke County,* 243.

45Thomas Barrett, physician and minister, was born in Anson County, North Carolina, on June 21, 1809. After residing in Missouri for a number of years, he moved with his family to Hopkins County, Texas, in 1848. He moved to Gainesville, Cooke County, in 1860. He began the practice of medicine in 1838 and was ordained later as a minister in the Disciples of Christ.

Barrett's account of the events narrated by Diamond, *The Great Hanging at Gainesville,* was the only known summary of those events from a contemporary observer, or participant, until George W. Diamond's chronicle in manuscript form came to light in 1962. (Publication of the Diamond account is made possible by the interest in Texas history of Mr. and Mrs. Harry Harlan of Dallas, Texas. Mrs. Harlan is a granddaughter of George W. Diamond.)

The Reverend Thomas Barrett wrote in 1885 that he was opposed to the hangings in 1862 and served on the "Citizens Court" under duress. As a result of threats arising from his lukewarm attitude, he felt it necessary to leave Gainesville shortly afterwards, moving to Vernon in 1863 and to Bell County in 1865. During the opening phases of Reconstruction in Texas he removed to Tennessee, where he remained

Hughes, Jas. Jones[46] and Thos. Wright,[47] whose appointments were unanimously confirmed by the meeting.

Resolved—That the committee thus constituted shall constitute a tribunal to be styled the "Citizens Court," which shall examine into all crimes and offenses committed in said co., and try saparatily [*sic*] all cases brought before it, hear the evidence, determine the guilt or innocence of the party accused and pronounce what punishment shall be inflicted.

Resolved—That the party accused shall in all cases be allowed to employ attorney and to send for and introduce such witnesses in his defense as he may desire, and may be confronted with any witness for or against him, and each witness shall be sworn by a Justice of the Peace, or other officer authorized by law to administer oaths.

Resolved—That the proceedings of said Court shall be private or kept secret so far as possible, from the enemy, and may at its discretion suppress any and all such testimony as may be deemed prudent and proper for the public safety.

Resolved—That the court shall be empowered to appoint a clerk & constable to assist in the transactions of its business, and may regulate the time of its own meetings and adjournments.

Resolved—Unanimously that we the citizens comprising this meeting pledge ourselves individually to sustain the proceedings of said Court and assist in carrying out its decisions in *all things*.

On motion the meeting adjourned. Wm. C. Young, Chm. James M. Peery, Secry.

---

until the end of 1866. Barrett then returned to Gainesville where he, with other members of the "Citizens Court," were subsequently tried and acquitted in civil court of any crime in connection with their participation in the work of the "Citizens Court." He continued the practice of medicine until 1878 and continued to preach until his death in Gainesville in 1892. Barrett, *The Great Hanging at Gainesville; Biographical Souvenir of the State of Texas*, 50-51.

[46]James Jones, born in North Carolina in 1812, took up land for farming in Cooke County after 1850. U. S. Eighth Census, 1860 (Returns of Schedule 1, Free Inhabitants, for Cooke County, Texas, microfilm, Dallas Public Library).

[47]Thomas Wright was born in North Carolina in 1812 and became a farmer in Cooke County sometime after 1850. He entered active military service of the Confederacy toward the end of the war, being named a second lieutenant in Captain James Hill's company of frontier guards on January 30, 1864. *Ibid.;* Smith, *First 100 Years in Cooke County*, 44.

CHARACTER OF COURT

The proceedings of this meeting furnish an unanswerable refutation of the charge that the Court was a self-constituted mob, and convince of their error [those] who had supposed that it was chosen by partisans in passionate haste and rashness. It was appointed after careful and mature deliberation and sustained by the calm and unimpassioned judgment of the people. It was composed of men selected from all portions of the co., not for their strong southern or secession predilections, or enmity toward Union men or those who would most likely be brought before them. But, on the other hand, they were chosen for their known moderation, intelligence and virtue as men and citizens.

What Texan, who is acquainted with the history of his country, does not revere the memory of Wm. C. Young, the talented, brave and generous spirit that presided over the meeting that appointed this Court? Who can attach to him who was so universally beloved, the ignoble purpose of attempting to sway its deliberations in a channel other than that in which a sense of duty and responsibility would naturally dictate? He offered himself a sacrifice to his country and but for the love he bore his State and his people, the writer would have been spared the penning of the bloodiest sequel of these pages.

What reader of Texas history is not familiar with the name of Montague, the chosen president of the Court? His name is associated with other scenes in the early history of his adopted State. And it is perpetuated & honored by being given to one of the counties of his adopted State in memory of his worth.

He was always distinguished whether in public or private life, his usefulness in the one only being excelled by his virtue in the other.

To show further in what estimation he was held by the people of Texas we copy the following, reproduced from an editorial in the Sherman Texas Courier, of date. Feby 1st 1874:[48]

[48]The date of this item from the Sherman *Texas Courier* included in Diamond's manuscript indicates that he completed it sometime after February 1, 1874. The

"MONTAGUE GROVE"

It is not genarally known by the newer portion of our citizens, that Sherman possesses a spot sacred to the commemoration of the early struggles of Texas. But such is the case. About two miles South of the square on the high prairie just to the right of the Mantua Road stands a grove of trees, covering several acres and plainly to be seen from the northern end of the city. This grove was the scene of a fierce Indian fight in the days of the Republic, some thirty years ago. The Indians, true to their instincts, had raided down upon the frontier—then several counties east of here, and had stolen all the horses they could drive off. There was no "Government policy" to interfere and a party of settlers headed by Daniel Montague, followed on their trail and overtook them about dusk one evening at said grove where Indians were camped, waiting until dark. They came down upon the unsuspecting Indians in style that only frontiersmen can, killed quite a number of them, recaptured their stock and learned the Indians a lesson that they remembered for years. Since then the place has been known as "Montague Grove," in honor of the leader of the whites, who before & afterwards by his heroism and bravery won many an honored place among Texas patriots. He was for many years a resident of the County which was named for him, but at the close of the late war he removed to Mexico, where we believe he has since died.

Rev. John W. Hamill was a shining light in the ministry—a gentleman of fine talents and of the highest integrity. He was for many years a missionary and Government agent among the Indians, and who accomplished much toward civilizing the untutored tribes and reconcile[d] them to a friendly relationship with the whites.

Rev. Thos. Barrett, the acknowledged head of the Christian Church denomination in Northwestern Texas, is a gentleman of

---

newspaper item itself recites that Montague moved to Mexico at the end of the "late war," with the editor adding, "where we believe he has since died."

Daniel Montague's return to North Texas and Cooke County in 1876 was a matter of widespread interest and a welcome surprise to the many who thought him dead. His death on December 20, 1876, at the home of his daughter, Mrs. Elizabeth Twitty, at Marysville, Cooke County, was widely reported throughout Cooke and adjoining counties, including Grayson County. It may be presumed, therefore, that George W. Diamond, then living at Whitesboro, Grayson County, completed the final draft of his account of the Great Hanging before the dramatic return and the actual death of Daniel Montague in 1876, or sometime between February 1, 1874, and December 20, 1876, at the latest.

rare intellectual endowments and highly distinguished for the religious culture of his mind.

Dr. Long is widely known as a physician of high standing in his profession.

The Jones' are men who rank among the most substantive citizens of Cooke County. Hughes' popularity has been tested by his election to the position of County Clerk in his County. Doss, Scanland, Simpson & Wright are all men of intelligence who stand high in the estimation of the people and [are] distinguished for their sobriety and good moral character.

In all the county of Cooke there could not have been twelve men selected who stand higher in the confidence and esteem of the people than the high-toned gentlemen who composed this court. It is believed they are all living yet, except the lamented president, Danl. Montague, and they still enjoy that same notoriety for honesty and integrity that characterized their lives at that time. So much then in refutation of the widespread rumor that the conspirators were hung by the rabble, or mob of lawless persons, who were prompted in their action by motives political, biggotry [*sic*] and revenge.

ORGANIZATION OF THE COURT

The court organized at once by appointing James M. Peery and R. G. Piper clerks and Wm. W. Bourland constable. The court was then sworn by R. G. Piper, chief Justice of Cooke County, to try all cases brought before it fairly & impartially, and render its decisions according to the evidence. Whereupon it was ordered by the Court that R. G. Piper, Aaron Hill, J. E. Shegog,[49] & Cincinnatus Potter[50] be appointed and constituted an examining committee, charged to examine witnesses [and] write down the evidence, first being sworn to discharge said duties impartially and to the best of their ability.

The bare mention of the names of the officers of the court among the people where known is a sufficient warrant for the intelligence and consciencious [*sic*] regard for truth and justice on the part of those selected by the Court to discharge their important duties, in obedience to its orders.

The Court, being organized, proceeded at once to the investigation of the cases reported ready for trial.

---

[49]A misspelling, apparently, of the name of J. A. Sheegog, who was born in Dublin, Ireland, in 1807. He appears to have emigrated to Texas about 1850, first having lived for a time in Tennessee and then in Louisiana. His occupation was farming. U. S. Eighth Census, 1860 (Returns of Schedule 1, Free Inhabitants, for Cooke County, Texas, microfilm, Dallas Public Library).

[50]Cincinnatus Potter was a farmer in Mississippi before he moved to Cooke County in 1858. One of the largest landholders in that section of the state, Potter also served as a county official and as commander of a company of the local militia organized to fight Indians. He later served as major in the state militia. Frank W. Johnson (Eugene C. Barker and E. W. Winkler, eds.), *A History of Texas and Texans* (5 vols.; Chicago, 1914), IV, 1681, 2072.

[TRIAL OF HENRY CHILDS]

The first prisoner brought before the Court was Dr. Henry Childs to whom reference has already been made.

THE PEOPLE AGAINST HENRY CHILDS	CONSPIRACY AND INSURRECTION

THE PRESIDENT—Dr. Henry Childs, you have been brought before this Court organized by the people of Cooke County charged with the crimes of conspiracy and insurrection; Have you any, or do you desire any counsel?

THE PRISONER—I have no counsel and deny that this court has jurisdiction in the case.

THE PRESIDENT. This Court is sustained in its jurisdiction by the unanimous voice of the people—are you ready for trial.

THE PRISONER—Probably as ready now as I shall ever be.

PRESIDENT—Listen to the reading of the charge—:

THE STATE OF TEXAS COUNTY OF COOKE	IN CITIZENS COURT OCT. 1ST 1862

In the name and by the authority of the people of the County of Cook [*sic*] and State of Texas, the citizens Court, duly selected, organized and sworn to examine and inquire into all crimes and offenses committed in said county and state aforesaid, on their oaths present; That on or about the 1st of September 1862 as well as long before and after that time, one Henry Childs, he then being a citizen of the county and state aforesaid, did commit the crime of treason in this that he did combine with other evil disposed persons, well knowing the design and intent of such combination, and did engage in and incite open and hostile opposition to the Civil Authorities of the said State and county, and attempted and advised resistance to the execution of the laws thereof. And that on the day and year aforesaid in the State and County aforesaid and before and after that time the said Henry Childs did commit the crime of conspiracy; in this that he did combine with other evil disposed persons, well knowing the design and intent of such combination, and did engage in and incite others to engage in and attempt to carry out the object of a certain order or organization, counselling [*sic*] and advising the killing of good citizens, the destruction of property, the disturbing of the public peace, contrary to the public safety and the peace and welfare of the people.

Danl Montague
Prest Citizen Court

PRESIDENT. Dr. Henry Childs— You have heard the charges preferred against you; what say you, guilty or not guilty.

PRISONER—Not guilty.

N. J. Chance Sworn

QUES. by the examining committee—Do you know anything concerning a secret organization in this country.

ANS. I know of such an order existing recently.

QUES. How did you obtain a knowledge of such organization.

ANS. By being initiated and receiving the signs, grips and passwords.

QUES. Do you know what was the object of said organization.

ANS. I know the objects which all the members initiated were sworn to carry out.

THE PRESIDENT. Please state to the court how you came to be initiated—and fully & particularly all the information you may have concerning said organization, giving the clerks time to write down your statements.

WITNESS. In the month of September last, while in conversation with Col. Bourland of this County, he informed me that he and others had received information concerning a secret organization in the country and that a council had been held privately in Gainesville, and upon consultation had chosen myself as the proper person to undertake to find out the secrets of said organization, and the names of those attached to it, as he informed me, for the purpose of saving the country from disturbance and violence, and bringing the members of the Order to justice.

Acting upon this suggestion, on the 26 day of September 1862, I started to Dr. Childs' residence. Meeting him on the road, I introduced myself, and after some conversation, he asked me if I was the Mr. Chance who had recently returned from the Southern Army. After answering him in the affirmative, he asked me a great many questions in regard to the Confederate Army, its numbers, situation, prospects.

I then remarked that a friend of mine had informed me that there was a secret union or peace party existing in the country and that he (Childs) was the very man to whom my friend had recommended me for full information on the subject. I told him, if there was such an organization as had been represented to me, it was the very thing I was hunting for. We then rode some distance together and dismounted when he informed me that If I desired to receive any communications from him I would be required to take an oath of secrecy. I requested him to proceed. He then administered to me the following oath: "You do solemnly swear in the presence of Almighty God, that you will forever keep secret the information now about to be communicated to you, so help you, God."

He then continued—"My friend—I propose to tell that ours is a secret organization existing in this country, and it is believed by all good men to be necessary for the protection of life and property. Its greatest good may not be realized or appreciated for awhile; but when the northern army comes into this country, and it most assuredly will in a very short time, this organization will be the means of saving the lives and the property of those attached to it & able to give the signs, grips and passwords."

I then asked him questions generally, concerning the origin and main objects of the organization. He replied that the Order had its origin in the necessity for organized resistance to the Confederate Conscript Law, and all laws passed by the so-called Confed. States without authority of the United States, and for the safety and protection of those who maintain the indestructibility of the Union. And sustained all means and measures of coercing the seceded states into obedience and subjection to the national authority, and that having conferred with military commandants in the Federal Army, the order through them had been circulated far and wide. That the design of the Organization was to avoid fighting against the North and on the first opportunity to rise in masse and fight the rebels and drive them out of the country and take their property. He then instructed me [in] the duties and obligations of the members and gave me, in detail, the plan of the order, saying in substance that each and every member of the order should recognize each other as brothers, and when any member should be arrested by the local authorities, all the other members were required to rally to his rescue, and set him at liberty.

He said that every member had more or less of ammunition, and it was the intention to organize to [*sic*] companies and seize some public ammunition then deposited at Gainesville and at Sherman, in Grayson County—that a time had been once fixed to capture the ammunition but it was concluded to postpone it for awhile. He said the ammunition was watched very closely by members of the order, and that it was impossible for the rebels to remove or conceal it. He said that they intended to act on one of two plans; first if the Northern Army came near and the militia should be ordered out from the border counties, they were to march into the ranks organized into companies and move on cheerfully until the ammunition should be issued, and the order of battle given, when they were to rally to themselves at a certain signal from the Northern Army, and turn their guns upon the rebels, and kill them or take them prisoner.

Secondly, if this plan should not be adopted, they intended to get all things ready at a very early day and before the militia were called out, hold meetings and set a time, and at a certain hour, march to the places where the ammunition was deposited and demand it civilly; if given up, all right—if not they were to take it by force of arms in retaliation against the rebels for seizing the forts, arsenals, arms & belongings to the United States. As soon as this was done they were to kill off the rebel party here, as there would be but few of them left, there being over two-thirds of the fighting male population of the country belonging to said order, except the soldiers then absent in the Confederate Army. He continued: "We will commence the fight here at home, against these rebels, if the Northern Army should not come in, and take such property as we may desire. Then, if unable to make a stand here long enough to cooperate with the Northern Army, we will start our families before us, and fight the rebels back until we reach the Federal lines. We have already sent messengers to our friends in the Federal Armies in Missouri and Kansas, to inform them of our contemplated movements, and assure them that a large majority of the men in this country are ready to join them, and fight by their side for the old Union and Constitution.

["]Some of the messengers have procured passports to go to St. Louis under the pretense of buying goods but their real object is to bear dispatches to the Federal Army concerning the condition of this country, and the strength of the order and its designs. We have signs, grips and passwords to distinguish us. And when the Federal Army comes in they will be recognized by, and they will know us as friends to their cause.["] I then requested him to give me those signs, grips and passwords. He replied, "I cannot do so unless you consent to be sworn again."

I requested him to state the nature of the oath. He then read over the obligation, which was written on a small piece of paper, and then informed me that if I did not wish to proceed further I could then withdraw and not be considered a member, but that the oath of secrecy must be kept sacred & invioble [*sic*]. I informed him that I had made application to him for initiation into the Order if it turned out as it had been represented to me; and discovering that so far it accorded with my feelings, I desired to proceed. He then administered to me the following oath: ["]You do solemnly swear in the presence of Almighty God, that you will use all your endeavors to reestablish the Old Constitution and Union, and to defend and protect every member of this Institution agt [*sic*] any arrest or seizure by the authorities of this State, and stand by them to the death; and if any of the members of this Order should be killed in their struggles to carry out its objects, you will do everything in your power to defend and protect their families, until otherwise provided for, so help you God."

He told me that the penalty for revealing any of the secrets of the Order was death, and in case any of the members should betray its existence and designs, it was solemnly enjoined upon every member to hunt him or them to the ends of the world. And that the most horrible death conceivable would be inflicted up[on] those guilty of treachery.

I asked him if he had any leading men in the Order. He replied, yes, many of them, and that [they] could be admitted and invested with the signs, grip & until they had taken the obligation above given that any persons, who might give me those signs, grip and passwords, was a full member, and that any information coming from such a source I might rely upon as being correct and legal. Here he gave me the signs, grip and passwords. (The witness here gave the Court the signs, grip and passwords as received from the accused.)

He remarked that the members of the Institution had been forced to take the oath of allegiance to the Confederacy, and that they did not consider it binding—that Jeff. Davis with his rebel army had, in their acts, been worse than murders and theives [*sic*]—that he and his army would soon be compelled to surrender; in no small degree, by the means and influence of the order—that the organization was spreading rapidly through the Southern Army—that they were six hundred strong in the city of Austin—that they were very strong in Grayson County; that a majority of the men in Sherman (except the soldiers) belonged the Order—that they were quite strong in Collin County, and in many counties in North Texas.

He then informed me that I might consider myself fully initiated and authorized to initiate others—such of my friends and acquaintances as I thought would do. I desired to have my brother, Joseph C. Chance, initiated. He regarded the proposition with serious doubts, saying my brother had been a rabbid [*sic*] secessionist and rebel. I allayed his apprehensions by telling him that my brother had changed in his political sentiments, and that he was willing and anxious to join. He gave me permission to initiate him. I requested him to do so, and on the following day he initiated my brother in my presence, repeating to him the same in substance, as have stated.

The prosecution here tendered the witness to the accused.

CROSS EXAMINED

QUES. by accused. How do you [know] that there was a secret organization as stated?

ANS. By being initiated by Dr. Henry Childs, representing himself as an initiating officer, from whom I learned the secrets, plans, etc.

QUES. Did you learn anything concerning this Order from any others of its members, if so, state what you heard.

ANS. I cannot say that I learned anything further than stated from other members, but I have the same signs, grip and password received from Dr. Childs given me by quite a number of men in this county. I answered the signs and was recognized as a member in good and regular standing. And since the arrest and the members of the Order have learned of my exposition of the plot, they have talked to me in prison freely, in regard to their plans and some of them stated they were initiated by the accused, Dr. Childs.

A. D. Scott[51] Sworn

QUES. Do you know of Dr. [Henry Childs].

ANSWER. I was sworn into this organization by Dr. Henry Childs. I took an obligation to keep secret all information given me and to fight for the establishment of the Old Constitution, and defend the members of the order and rescue them from prison. He gave me the signs, grip and password, and said the punishment of revelation was certain death. He said the object was to drive the rebels out of the country or kill them, and that the first thing to do was to get possession of plenty of ammunition—that there was a quantity of powder in Gainesville and a load on the way from Jefferson and probably had arrived in Sherman. I do not remember the day I was initiated. Dr. Childs stated the attack might be made the next night to get the powder. He said the signs would protect us when the Northern Army should come in, and enable the members to act together in any emergency.

THE COURT. Dr. Henry Childs, Do you know of a secret organization in this county, of the character referred to by the witness.

ANS. I know there is a secret organization in this country organized for the purpose of protecting life and property and to prevent the shedding of blood, mobs, Jay-hawking, etc.

---

[51]A. D. Scott, one of the prisoners tried before the "Citizens Court," was born in Kentucky in 1821 and came to Texas, probably by way of Tennessee, sometime before 1860. U. S. Eighth Census, 1860 (Returns of Schedule 1, Free Inhabitants, for Cooke County, Texas, microfilm, Dallas Public Library), family no. 389.

QUES. Does this organization have signs, grips and passwords by which the members know each other?

ANS. It has not.

The testimony here closed, the prisoner is found guilty and the accused remanded to prison.

Being brought before the Court a second time to receive his sentence, he requested the privilege of correcting his former statements. Being again sworn he deposed as follows:

"There are signs, grips and passwords in the Order which will afford protection when the Northern Army comes in, and by which the members know each other["].

THE COURT. Henry Childs, you have been tried upon the charges preferred against you, by twelve men selected from among your neighbors, and by them you have been found guilty. This court has endeavored to extend to you every right and privilege known to the laws of the laws of the County. That it has acted fairly and impartially in all its proceedings, and has shown no disposition to abuse the extraordinary powers granted to it by the people, themselves your neighbors, we feel assured will not be questioned by any one, not even yourself. We feel the grave responsibility resting upon us and have pursued with solemn and melancholly [*sic*] step the path of duty assigned us. Although our proceedings have been conducted in the midst of considerable confusion and excitement, we have not shared its influences to that extent privileged to those who have lighter and much less serious obligations to discharge to the people. Those on the outside have performed their duty—Ours yet remains to be done. Theirs was a duty of *actions*. Ours is a question of conscience. Theirs was a matter of personal safety, while ours involves the life or death of a fellowman, our neighbor. Having discharged their duty faithfully, we must discharge ours conscienciously [*sic*]. You were duly notified of the charges preferred against you, and on the trial was confronted with all the witnesses against you. The truth of their statements you did not only fail or attempt to disprove, but now come before us and acknowledge them correct. And if true and correct, they place you beyond the protection of any law known to the civilization of the present day. In the discharge of our last said duty to the people, let us assure you that you may not expect reprieve or extenuation of the judgment now about to be pronounced, and while it is yet time, may you use it in an assiduous effort to prepare for Eternity. This world is but of to-day—the one beyond, that of forever; and may you, in expiating the crimes against the laws of mankind, propitiate and appease the anger [*sic*] offended majesty of the Great Lawgiver of the Universe. In accordance therefore, with the decision of this Court, you will be taken from your place of confinement, on the 4th day of

October '62 between the hours of 12 and 2 o'clock of said day, and hung by the neck until you are dead, and may God have mercy on your soul.

The prisoner listened to the sentence attentively, without seeming to fully appreciate or comprehend its meaning in all its terrible reality. Though evincing much concern at the strange and peculiar surroundings he appeared not to realize his situation, and the full import of the fatal words addressed to him. This strange indifference may reasonably be attributed to the novelty of the proceedings, and a still bouyant hope that some fortuitous circumstance would intervene in his favor, and screen him from the gallows.

Being the first one tried, he was not aware of the determined and resolute character of the tribunal which had condemned him to death. He probably cherished the delusive hope of rescue or deliverance until brought to the place of execution.

EXECUTION OF DR. HENRY CHILDS

Full preparations having been made previously, he was taken in an open carriage surrounded by the guards to a large widespreading elm tree, about one half mile East of the town of Gainesville, which then formed the centre of a large concourse of citizens resting upon a file of soldiers forming a hollow square. In sad and gloomy silence the cortege moved slowly through the rushing, crowding throngs of people, the carriage finally halting immediately under a large strong limb branching out at right angles from the trunk of the giant elm. To this limb a rope was attached and the pendent end adjusted around the neck of the condemned man. In the meantime he began to realize his situation and to feel the force of the address of the president of the Court. The mockeries of this world began to fade from before his view and the dim outline of the new and unknown to peer above the horizon of Time's limited boundaries. The prospect of so sudden a change shook his strong frame with fear; while pale and trembling he listened to the last earthly voice, a death knell, sounding the

Warrant of Execution

The People Against Henry & Ephraim Childs	Conspiracy Insurrection

Capt. A. Boutwell.[52] You are hereby authorized and commanded in the name and by the authority of the people of the County of Cooke and State of Texas to take into custody the body of Henry Childs and him safely keep until the 4th day of October 1862, and at 2 o'clock p.m. on said day you will execute the sentence of this Court, by hanging the said Henry Childs by the neck until he is dead dead dead. And may God have mercy on his soul.

Danl Montague, Prest.

The carriage was then driven from beneath the limb, and in a

[52]Alexander Boutwell, the first sheriff of Cooke County, was born in Arkansas in 1825. He was a member of the Peters Colony and took up land as a farmer in Cooke County before its organization in 1848. Connor, *The Peters Colony of Texas*, 197; Smith, *First 100 Years in Cooke County*, 13; U. S. Seventh Census, 1850 (Returns of Schedule 1, Free Inhabitants, for Cooke County, Texas, microfilm, Dallas Public Library), family no. 2.

moment more the body of Henry Childs dangled in the air, while the branches of the obstinate and unyielding elm trembled like an aspen under the weight and shuddering motion of the dying man.

After life became extinct the body was taken down and placed in possession of the weeping family and friends, who with appropriate ceremonies gave it decent sepulture.

Thus died Dr. Henry Childs. He came from Missouri to Texas, but a few year anterior to the War between the States and was regarded by his neighbors as a man of upright deportment, and possessing a degree of intelligence above mediocrity. It cannot be said of him, however, that his conduct & associations were of that kind to warrant an opinion in his favor, beyond a mere negative conception of the man as an individual having the mind undecided as to his character.

His countenance was of that peculiar cast, calculated to create vague conjecture as to whether he might be a man prone to good or evil. About forty two or three years of age, stout [of] build though not corpulent; shoulders slightly stooped, brown hair, and blue eyes, he seemed the embodiment of good health, and but for his connection with this "Order," might have lived an honorable and useful life.

After he had sworn in Col. Chance, he was told by his best friends & members that they were fearful that he had dug the pit for their destruction—that they feared Chance's treachery, knowing him better than he (Childs) could possibly know him. He persisted that Chance had been sufficiently wrought upon to change his mind, and that he entertained no question of his good faith and integrity. After being arrested he talked freely with Col. Chance & appeared to harbor no ill will or revenge against him.

He made no confession of guilt, beyond a determined purpose to resist all Confederate laws and to aid the Northern Army whenever an opportunity offered, let it cost what it might in carrying out such a purpose. He indicated no disposition to communicate anything regarding the "Order," and though positively denying that it had signs, grips and passwords, without any interference on the part of others, requested the privilege of withdrawing this statement and giving an affirmative answer to the question. It had never been ascertained what induced him to make this statement willfully false, and afterwards desire to correct it. He died with the secret in his soul, and is known only to the great Searcher of all hearts.

Drawing the mantle of charity over his deeds and his life, let his body rest beneath the green prairie sod, in peace, and let those who cherish a memory of his faults also remember that; To err is human—to forgive, divine.

COL. N. J. CHANCE

The testimony of Col. Chance, while applying directly in the trial of Dr. Henry Childs, sheds much light upon the whole plot of the conspirators.

From his evidence, it is plain to be seen that he was the right man for the discharge of the hazardous work assigned him. From first to last he stood by the citizens, and to his caution, courage and integrity may in a great measure be attributed the success of the plans to check the progress of the "Order." He was a man of only a short residence in Texas, but volunteered in the Confederate service at the beginning of the war. Possessing a sound and discriminating judgment, he was nevertheless uneducated. He was quite communicative in his disposition, and in his intercourse with friends frank, open and candid. Kind in his nature and generous beyond his capacity to give and bestow.

Many of the accused called him to their side while in prison to ask his advice, and to aid them in presenting their defense to the Court, while many under the gallows addressed their last words to him as a friend, none seeming to remember him as the prime author of their ruin.

At the close of the war, many speculations were indulged in on the subject of the dangerous position he occupied, many prophesying that he would fall a sacrifice to the revenge of those whom he had betrayed. But so far from this being the case, no citizen seemed more indifferent upon the subject of his personal safety; though in a short time after quiet had been restored, he with his family and brother removed northward. In giving his testimony before the Court, the accused would give his statements the closest attention, and in no instance did they attempt to deny his answers. They all accorded to him honesty and veracity.

[TRIAL OF] EPHRAIM CHILDS

Ephraim Childs, brother of Dr. Henry Childs, the first member of the order to uncautiously and unwittingly expose its existence and designs, was the second brought before the Court for trial. He was regarded as among the zealous and active members of the "Organization" and was often appealed to for counsel and assistance when the interests of the organization were in any way involved. His over-zealous conduct and premature revelations of the designs of the "Institution" opened the way to detection and final ruin of himself, his brother & his friends.

THE PEOPLE VERSUS EPHRAIM CHILDS	CONSPIRACY AND INSURRECTION

Being brought before the Court and the charges read, he entered the plea of not guilty.

J. B. McCurley sworn.

[WITNESS.] Some time in the month of September last, I met the accused at the hotel in the town of Gainesville, Cooke County, Texas. He asked me if I did wish to go into a society for the good of the country, and continued by asking me if I were not a good Union man. I told him I had been one. He then said let us go into the room. It may be you are one still. After entering the room he gave me signs, which I did not understand, and of course could not answer them. He walked out of the room, remarking "You know nothing about it." He said if I desired to know all about it, his brother, the doctor, was one of the head men in the Society, and would take pleasure in initiating me. He stated that these d——d rebels about town (and there were a good many of them), had a large quantity of powder, and that they intended to have it. And that very soon. He said the order had signs grips and passwords by which they knew each other and that the order was spreading rapidly, & insisted that I should see his brother and be initiated.

W. W. Reeder Sworn.

[WITNESS.] Ephraim Childs informed me that his brother, Dr. Henry Childs, was invested with full authority to initiate persons into this secret organization. He gave me the signs, grip and password. (Witness then gave them to the Court, which were recognized as being those of the "Order.")

Dr. Henry Childs Sworn.

[WITNESS.] I initiated my brother, E. Childs, into this secret Order, of my own choice, and gave him the signs, grip and password.

A volume of evidence might be introduced to show the active connection of Ephraim Childs with the "Order." The main features of the testimony in this case being about the same as those exhibited on the trial of Dr. Childs, it is not deemed necessary to repeat here, in detail, the long and connected chain of circumstances which placed the accused beyond the hope of acquital [*sic*].

DECISION OF THE COURT

The prisoner, Ephraim Childs, is found guilty, and is sentenced to be hung on the 4th day of October 1862 at 2 o'clock p.m. of said day until he is dead.

Daniel Montague
Prest Citizens Court

DEATH WARRANT

Capt. A. Boutwell: You are hereby authorized and commanded in the name and by the authority of the people of the County Cooke and State of Texas to take into custody the body of Ephraim Childs and him safely keep until the 4th day of October 1862, and at 2 o'clock p.m. of said day you will execute the sentence of this Court, by hanging the said E. Childs by the neck until he is dead.

Daniel Montague
Prest. Cit. Ct.

While sentence was being pronounced he remained quiet and apparently unmoved by the solemn warning given him by the venerable president. Like his brother, he remained true to the oaths he had taken and refused to make any confession or statements regarding the order, as he had been advised to do by many of his fellow prisoners.

He was several years the junior of his brother, and a man decidedly more affable and companionable. He was a man of strong will, obstinate and unyielding when opposed, and dangerous when angry. He appeared, as did his brother, to take no notice of his critical situation until near the closing scene of his mortal existence.

[TRIAL OF A. D. SCOTT]

THE PEOPLE versus A. D. SCOTT	CONSPIRACY AND INSURRECTION

THE PRESIDENT—A. D. Scott—You have been brought before this Court charged with the crimes of conspiracy and insurrection. Are you now ready to hear these charges read and defend yourself against them?

ACCUSED. I am ready to be tried, though I have no defense to make.

After the reading of the charges and questions as to his guilt or innocence, he said:

I belong to a secret order known by its members as a Union party. I know of no other object than that we were to fight for the Union, & in doing so, were to take possession of the country, and kill those at home who did not favor our purpose, as I stated in my evidence on the trial of Dr. Henry Childs.

I engaged generally in the meetings and took part in the business of the Order generally. My understanding was that we were to resist the Conscript law, and all laws passed by Confederate authority. I do not know what was the object or intention of others, only as I obtained information on the subject of the order in our meetings. I received the signs, grip and password. This is all I know in regard to the Order. And if I am judged guilty by these statements, why, then I am guilty. If these statements condemn me, I shall not regret that I made them. I make them voluntarily, and desire that they may be used only against myself, without prejudicing the cause of others.

THE PRESIDENT. Then do you want the Court to understand that you plead guilty to the charges.

THE PRISONER. I wish the Court to understand the statements I have made, and if they sustain the charges I have no doubt that the Court will adjudge me guilty. I not I hope to be released [*sic*].

THE PRES. Do you wish to introduce any witnesses in your defense.

PRISONER. I do not. I see no use in introducing any testimony in my own behalf, as it would be impossible to obtain the evidence of any witness better acquainted with the facts than myself, and they are as I have stated to the Court.

He was found guilty and sentenced to be hung. Arriving at the place of execution he confessed his guilt and exhorted the people to continue their work to break up the "Order," which had so ignominiously terminated his existence.

He viewed calmly the preparations for his execution. And when the last awful moment arrived he jumped heavily from the carriage; and falling near three feet, dislocated his neck, he died without the violent contraction of a single muscle.

[TRIAL OF] M. D. HARPER

THE PEOPLE vs. M. D. HARPER	CONSP. & INS.

After hearing the charges read, and being asked the usual questions, he answered, "Not guilty."

Henry Childs Sworn.

[WITNESS.] I was initiated into this secret organization by the accused, M. D. Harper. He told me what the designs of the Order were, what it proposed to accomplish & what it ultimately hoped to attain—the overthrow of the Confederacy, and the establishment of the Old Union and Constitution.

W. W. Johnson Sworn.

[WITNESS.] I belong to a secret society. My first information of the order was received from Enoch Welch, who told me I could get into the Society by applying to the prisoner, M. D. Harper. I visited Mr. Harper in company with Welch, and I requested him to tell me all about the organization, its objects, etc.

He said, above all things, we were to stand by and take care of each other and if any of the members should be arrested or taken up, we were to rescue them. He said we were to bring this war to a close—and said something about reinstating the old Constitution. He then administered to me an oath to keep secret everything told me. I took another oath finally but do not know exactly what it was. I will say as near as I can that the oath was to band together for self defense against the secessionists, protect each other and hunt down any traitor to the cause. He gave me signs, grips and passwords. I heard some hints of a correspondence between the Northern Army and our Order, and was told by Harper that the signs were to protect the members when the Northern Army came into the country. We were to get ammunition at Gainesville, Sherman and fight our way out of Texas if we could not hold the country. If we could hold the country, the rebels were to be killed or driven out, and we were to take possession of their property.

At this stage of the proceedings the Court adjourned, and upon meeting again Harper made full confession of his guilt. He said:

I entertain the highest respect for the opinion and judgment of this Court. I sincerely acquit you of any attempt to do me any injustice and commend you to the confidence of my neighbors and yours for this fearless performance of your duty. I humbly beg your forgiveness and the pardon of those whom I may have wronged by my connection with this order.

I done all in my power to further and promote its objects. I was a Union man and desired the restoration of the old government, and I am now grieved to know that my efforts to resist the march of secession have led to results ruinous to the peace and happiness of the community in which I live.

I did not think a desire or an honest effort to reestablish the Union could be termed criminal; but the order soon discovered that its organization would result in failure unless certain steps were taken to reach the end contemplated. The measures adopted to carry out its designs, I am sorry to say, if successful, would have terminated in crime and bloodshed, and the destruction of property.

I hope the people will forgive me for aiding and advising the cause pursued by the order, though many of its acts and the conduct of many individuals I did not approve. I can only say that I deeply regret the past and, if spared, I hope to strive to redeem my character by better conduct in future.

He was found guilty and listened to the reading of his sentence with calm and stolid indifference, but when retiring from the court-room he assumed an excited and defiant appearance, exhibiting the true character of his disposition—bold, determined and undaunted in time of peril. Although about forty-five or fifty years of age, he had little of his manhood. He was tall, rawboned, strong and active for a man of his age; and being resolute and uncompromising in whatever he undertook, he was regarded as one of the main pillars of the society. He was very officious and active in his duties as a member of the "Order," as will appear hereafter on the trial of others. His arrest caused several meetings of the different companies to systematize a plan for his release; but the scheme failed in consequence of the prompt organization of the citizens

Like Dr. Childs and others who were convicted and hung, he seemed to place his reliance in the success of the Union Army and to console himself in his crimes with the reflection that no act could be termed criminal per se which was the necessary result of a purpose to aid the Federal Army in reestablishing the old Constitution and Union. He hints this belief very strong in his statement to the Court. To this shrewd subterfuge to avoid conviction he was probably indebted to Dr. Childs, for while Childs was much less active and zealous than Harper, he done the thinking for those acquainted with him, while they done the work of the order. Childs, after being condemned by the testimony of unimpeached witnesses, clearly connecting him with the darkest designs of the conspirators, could only say in his testimony against Harper that he only told of a purpose to overthrow the Confederacy and reestablish the Union. Childs being initiated into the "Order" by Harper, and only instructing him to the extent stated by him to the Court.

At this trial of Harper, does it not appear strange to any sound mind that Childs should give in detail the designs and the objects of the "Order" more comprehensive as well as more heinous in their character? This version of the order of things would present the strange anomaly of the creation being endowed with more power than the creator. Harper did tell Johnson however, that they were to kill the rebels or drive them out of the country, and take their property. Upon the evidence of Johnson and the confessions of the prisoner himself, the Court could only do as it did and find him guilty and sentence him to be hung.

After the bodies of Henry and Ephraim Childs had been removed, Harper was conducted to the place of execution and there in the midst of a multitude of people and a weeping family remained unmoved, and obeying the directions of the executioner in a business-like manner stepped off the carriage, and in a minute more nothing but the perishing mortality of M. D. Harper was left on earth.

Whatever his errors or crimes may have been, let his dust rest in peace, and a spirit of sincere remission linger about his house and lowly bed.

[TRIAL OF HENRY FIELDS]

THE STATE VS. HENRY FIELDS (SHOE MAKER)	DISLOYALTY, & TREASON.

Henry Childs sworn.

[WITNESS.] I iniated [*sic*] the prisoner Henry Fields into this organization.

J N. Helm sworn.

[WITNESS.] In a conversation with Henry Fields recently he stated that he was in favor of the North. On one occasion he said, if the Conscript Law was raised to include men of his age, he would hang before he would fight. I remarked that if he should see the rope coming, he might probably change his mind.

He replied, "I would hang." He also stated, that he endorsed the proclamation issued by Maj. Genl. Butler, U.S. Army, upon his occupation of the city of New Orleans. I borrowed a newspaper containing said proclamation from the prisoner, who requested me to return it as he wished some of his family to read it.

THE PRISONER. I do not belong to a secret organization having for its objects the overthrow of the Confederate Government and the reestablishment of the Old Union.

Being brought before the Court a second time, he deposed as follows:

["]I was partially initiated by Dr. Childs, but refused to take the degree in full; but afterwards did go through."

He was found guilty, and hung.

Fields was called by his neighbors a *clever* man, and a useful citizen. His implication in this secret and wicked plot astonished the people, more perhaps, than any others.

After being sentenced he made full confession of his guilt. When brought to the place of execution, addressing Col. Chance, he said:

I am guilty of the charges against me. I am guilty of whatever criminality may be attached to this organization. I am guilty of disloyalty and treason against this government, of a purpose to subvert and destroy it.

The punishment before me seems awful to him who is about to suffer it. But it is due for the crimes I have committed. My crimes have been many and great; and I am sorry, that they have been so great that I cannot hope to obtain forgiveness from the injured people. I think the people and jury have done their duty, so far. I hope they will continue their work, until every one that belongs to this order shall be brought to justice.

Tell the Jury their verdict is a just one approved by me and sanctioned by high Heaven. Tell them, I thank them, and accuse them of no injustice; but, that I acquit them, as I do all mankind, of any wrong done me.

I hope the people will not remember my transgressions against those who bear my name, and are attached to me, by kindred ties. Let them rather favor the kind offices of charity in washing away the stain and rewarding memory with whatever virtue there is in the deepest contrition of spirit; try to forget how I have lived, but remember that at least I *died* humbled and pentinent.

His last words to the people, were: "Go on with the work you have so fearlessly begun."

[TRIAL OF I. W. P. LOCK]

THE STATE vs. I W. P. LOCK	DISLOYALTY & TREASON

I. H. Mounts[53] sworn.

[WITNESS.] I was sworn into this society, by I. W. P. Lock. At the same time, he swore in P Q Russell, Wm Anderson,[54] George Anderson, John Tourly, and Richard Anderson.

E. F. Anderson sworn.

[WITNESS.] I know of a secret organization in this country. The prisoner, Wm Lock, told me it was to afford us protection when the Northern Army should come in. Mr. Lock gave me the signs, grip, and password. Lock told me that we were to get powder at Sherman. The design of the organization, was the reconstruction of the old Constitution, and Union.

THE PRISONER. Jackson Mount swore me and I swore him into this organization. I introduced the password "Arizina," and the signs, and grips of the order. Mount and myself were the first starters of this order. I have heard that there was an organization to break up both armies. I have heard since that it was the same as this; and that the signs and password would protect us when the Northern army come.

Mount and myself took two oaths. We were to kill, or assist in killing, every man who should reveal either the existence of the order or its plans and designs. I advised my men, (Lock had a company,) not to go to the war.

Dr Eli Thomas sworn.

[WITNESS.] In a conversation with the prisoner last night (in person) I made a *clean breast* of the whole matter. Lock said he had scruples about doing so himself, on account of the oaths he had taken in the order.

He was found guilty and hung.

---

[53]A misspelling, apparently, of the name of Jackson H. Mounts, a member of the Peters Colony who moved to Texas before 1844. He was born in Illinois in 1823. He was a resident of Collin County in 1850, being listed in the census for that year as family no. 312. Connor, *The Peters Colony of Texas*, 347.

[54]A "William Anderson," twenty seven-year-old farmer born in Tennessee, is listed in the U. S. Eighth Census, 1860 (Returns of Schedule 1, Free Inhabitants, for Cooke County, Texas, microfilm, Dallas Public Library).

After he was condemned, his fellow prisoners urged him to confess his guilt and make a *clean breast* of it, as most of them had done. He was sufficiently wrought upon to induce him to send for a minister of the Gospel to advise him in the matter. He sent for the Rev. Wm. Hamill and the Rev Mr Barrett, both members of the Jury. He laid before [them] the oaths he had taken, his action under them already developed, and the state of his mind in reference to a revelation of all the plans and designs of the "Order."

They assured him that they did not desire to sit upon such a delicate question; it being as far from their wish, as from their competency to decide matters of conscience for other men—that they, also, were members of the tribunal who had condemned him to die, which fact, alone, seemed [to] be sufficient to disqualify them for such a delicate trust. He refused to entertain these excuses saying; that he had ever known them to be good men and, more recently while on trial for his life, he had discovered them to be men of upright judgments, and he believed had done Justice between him and the country.

They told him that the crime for which he had been condemned consisted in *going into* the society, that the crime consisted in taking the oaths, in the first instance; and in no wise could he be held responsible, as a moral being, for *going out* of the order, no matter what revelations might become necessary in his abandonment of an association which, by the laws of the land, had been held to be criminal and desperately wicked. With this, they introduced the doctrine of repentence as taught by the Bible and left him a victim to his own melancholly [*sic*] reflections.

He continued from time to time, to defer making any revelations until the hour arrived for his execution; and notwithstanding the repeated efforts to relieve his mind of any doubts as to his moral obligation to reveal the names and secrets of the "Order," he died with his fidelity to the cause only partially shaken.

His own statements before the Jury were disconnected and evidently showed a disposition to evade the truth. He spoke boastingly of himself as being the author of the main secrets of the order; but afterwards admitted that he *heard* the signs, grip, and password were the same in the Northern wing of the "Order."

From other facts, it is clearly ascertained that he is not entitled to the distinction he claims in the order. His conduct throughout revealed all the elements of a depraved nature, and he died upon the tree exhibiting that defiance of death that usually seizes hold on the last moments of a depraved, wicked, and abandoned heart.

[TRIAL OF W. W. MORRIS]

THE STATE vs. W. W. MORRIS[55]	DISLOYALTY & TREASON

[THE ACCUSED] plead [*sic*] guilty, making the following statement to the jury:

I was initiated into this secret organization by M. D. Harper. This organization has for its object the reconstruction of the old Constitution and Union of the United States. I was sworn to secrecy, in the first place, with old man Wernell and Floyd. And, secondly, I was sworn to do every thing in my power to reconstruct the old Union and reinstate the old Constitution Harper gave us the signs, grip, and password. He informed us that the organization originated in the Northern Army, and was sent South. He told us of the plot to procure powder at Sherman. We were told that we would not have to fight against the North. The powder was to be used against the South.

He was found guilty and hung.

55"Wesley Morris," thirty-two-year-old farmer born in Tennessee, and "William Morris," fifty-year-old farmer born in Georgia, are listed in the 1860 federal census for Cooke County. *Ibid.*

[TRIAL OF RICHARD ANDERSON]

The State vs. Richard Anderson	Disloyalty & Treason

The evidence against this prisoner being the same in substance as that against Harper & Lock, it is deemed unnecessary to repeat it here. He was found guilty, and after [being] sentenced to be hung, made full confession of his guilt.

[TRIAL OF ELI THOMAS]

THE STATE vs. ELI THOMAS[56]	DISLOYALTY & TREASON,

The testimony against Dr. Thomas being the same as in the foregoing trials, he was found guilty, and after being sentenced to die, he addressed the Court the following letter:

Gainesville Texas
Oct 18th 1862

To the Honorable Court of
Inquiry, sitting at Gainesville

I request the Honorable Court to reconsider my case. The evidence given by Wett, if given correctly, would be decidedly in my favor. If I were permitted to appear in Court with Wett, Peters, Hays & Crisp, I think I could convince the Court that I am not so bad a man as the Court takes me to be.

The intention of others, I cannot help. I want every man brought to justice; and will pledge myself to do all that I can to search into, and expose, the low cunning of man, if I am released. I am willing to have 'Squire Martin,' 'Squire Helm' and others of my neighbors to look at my former conduct. My last will and testament is that I will be true to my Country.

My interest is here. My protection is the law, and I intend to be subject to the laws that be; for it is ordained of God. My book teaches this. If I have had bad designs, I call upon God to take that part from me; which he has promised to do, to those who love him.

Eli Thomas

Before his death, he confessed his guilt, and entreated the other prisoners to do the same thing; telling them that it was an awful thing to die, but more awful still to die with a lie in their mouths.

---

[56]Dr. Eli Thomas, a physician born in Ohio in 1823, moved to Cooke County prior to 1860. He had lived previously in Kentucky and Iowa. *Ibid.*

[TRIAL OF EDWARD HAMPTON AND JOHN A. MORRIS]

THE STATE vs. EDWARD HAMPTON AND JOHN A. MORRIS	DISLOYALTY & TREASON

The testimony in these cases is the same as in its preceding trials. They were all found guilty by the Court, and at the gallows they acknowledged their crimes, and exhorted the people to continue the work to break up the order that had so ignominiously terminated their existence.

[TRIAL OF JOHN M. CRISP]

THE STATE vs. JOHN M CRISP[57]	DISLOYALTY & TREASON

Eli Thomas sworn.

[WITNESS.] John M. Crisp swore me into a secret organization having for its object the reconstruction of the old Constitution and Union. He gave me the signs, grip and password.

Crisp, himself, when brought at before the Court, admitted that he had been initiated into the organization. Pending his trial, he addressed the Court the following letter;

Fully believing this to be the last time that I will be permitted to communicate with the Honorable tribunal by which I am to be tried, I adopt this method to do so; and for this reason: Having never before been brought before a Court, and my natural disposition and constitutional powers being so framed, the presence of that august body has the effect to scatter my mind. And while in your presence I cannot collect my thoughts, I will now make in writing these further statements in behalf of my injured Country:

Some time in the month of August, 1862, Dr Thomas, and Parson Baker, came to my shop; and being there a short time, went out and seated themselves some distance from me. They returned and requested me to initiate him (Thomas), I understanding him to mean, to enter as a member into the Secret institution to reinstate the old Constitution, I refused, pointing to Baker, [and] told him to get Baker to do it. Thomas laughed, and said no; but for me to do it. I told him I was awkward but would do the best I could. Not having a regular form of oath, I framed one, in like manner, as I have stated before your Honors heretofore; giving him the signs, grip, and password. Parson Baker and myself, about one week before the above stated time, were initiated by Dr McCarty. McCarty told Baker he could initiate also.

A few days after this I was informed that each member had the right to initiate his neighbor. I have initiated six persons, in all, to-wit: Sam'l Crisp, H. J. Essman, Eli Hinkle, I. M. Baily, Mansell Baily, and Dr Eli Thomas. I suppose Essman and Hinkle are not yet ar-

[57]John M. Crisp, a blacksmith, emigrated to Texas, probably by way of Missouri, prior to 1860. He was born in Kentucky in 1824. *Ibid.*, family no. 407.

rested. Dr Thomas informed me that he had initiated an old man, by the name of Parson Howard.

I desire to explain one other thing, which I named to one of your honorable body just as I left the jury room. James Harryman came to my house the day before I was arrested and informed me that they had held a secret meeting, and said that Capt. Garrison, or Lock, had been to a Mr Love's in the Chicasaw [*sic*] Nation and had initiated him; and that he had plenty of powder that the order could have whenever they wanted it. And now, I acknowledge my wrong and implore you that while examining the testimony I have given, if I have, or seemed to quibble, I pray you to remember the situation of my mind, and deal with me in mercy.

John M. Crisp

After being condemned, he again addressed the Court as follows:—

Gainesville, Oct. 18th 1862

To the Honorable Court
now in session, at Gainesville:

Whereas, through the mercies of Almighty God, and the Court, my life has been prolonged to this present time, I greatly desire the patience of the Court, yet a little longer.

I hope the Court will condescend to hear my imperfect petition and offered obligations to my injured country. I do not expect to influence you; but implore you, for mercy—that my life may be spared.

First, if in your wisdom and mercy you see fit to spare my life, and I ever again show any signs of not being true to our Southern Confederacy, then I will not plead for mercy any more; but will submit my life, to pay the forfeit.

Secondly, I desire to be placed under the watch-care of some of our truest and best Southern men, that they may from time to time examine into my conduct; and if they find any thing wrong, report me forthwith.

Thirdly, I am willing and anxious at any time to do any thing in my power to sustain the independence of our Country. And forthly, if we can have any correct of the future by the past, I would refer your honorable body to Capt. Roff, Harry Howeth, W. B. Magill, Joseph Martin, Wm. West, and Charles Hibert, and let them say what my actions have been heretofore in giving aid to the volunteers. I now submit by begging your forgiveness for the wrongs which I may have done; and I promise you that if my life is spared, I will never commit wrong again.

John M. Crisp

He was hung in accordance with the sentence of the Court and, no doubt from the record before us, died a much better man than he had lived.

[TRIAL OF SAMUEL CARMICHAEL]

THE STATE VS. SAMUEL CARMICHAEL[58]	DISLOYALTY & TREASON

It is in evidence that Carmichael was well informed as to the objects and purposes of the organization, but the testimony does not develop the fact that he was ever sworn in. When the detail was made to go to Fort Cobb during the Indian excitement in that quarter, Carmichael peremptorily refused to go, saying that he would fight to the death at home, first.

He was an outspoken enemy to the South and, in every way, considered a dangerous and bad man in Society. He was found guilty and hung.

---

[58]Samuel Carmichael, a carpenter born in Tennessee in 1821, settled in Cooke County prior to 1860. He probably had moved to Texas by way of Alabama. *Ibid.*, family no. 33.

[GROUP TRIAL]

The State vs. C. A. Jones, ("hump back") James Powers ("carpenter") Eli M. Scott, Thomas Baker ("old man") Geo. W. Anderson, Abraham McNeese, Henry Cochran ("30"), C. F. Anderson, Wm Wernell, B. F. Barnes ("35 or 40") Wm Rodes, and N. M. Clark ("25")	Disloyalty, & Treason

The testimony against the above mentioned conspirators corresponds with the testimony herein before produced on the trial of Childs, Fields, Harper, Lock, and others. They all acknowledged their connection with the organization, and made full confession of their guilt at the gallows.

[TRIAL OF RAMEY DYE]

The State vs. Ramey Dye.[59]	Disloyalty or Treason

Arphax Dawson[60] Sworn

[Witness.] Ramey Dye came to my house and told me that M. D. Harper had been arrested on the charge of being connected with our society; and that there would be a meeting held that night, (1st Oct. 1862) near Lattimer's and Richie's steam mill, for the purpose of consulting how to rescue Harper. He wished me to attend and bring my gun, which I did. The meeting was attended by Ramey Dye, John M. Wiley,[61] Isham Welch,[62] Wm Boyles,[63] John Ware, H. Gilman, Robt Duncan and others.
He talked about the rescue of Harper. We came to the conclusion that the force at Gainesville was too strong for us to accomplish our purpose.

Ben F. Barnes sworn.

[Witness.] There was a meeting at Steam Mill last Wednesday night. Some members observed we had better go to the Northern army where we could fare better. They were to hold a meeting the next night, somewhere. Ramey Dye was appointed captain. The meeting was to be held in the bottom of Jordan Creek, near Alveads.

I. W. Morris sworn.

[Witness.] I was at the meeting at Richie's Mill. Dr. Foster said the object of the meeting was to rescue Harper; and he wanted

---

59Ramey Dye, a farmer, was born in Kentucky in 1819 and migrated to Cooke County sometime before 1860. The author of this narrative noted beside Dye's name in the manuscript: "Guarded the others (prisoners) for several days." *Ibid.*

60Arphax Dawson was born in Georgia in 1805. He was one of the first settlers in Cooke County. His daughter Mary was married to Ramey Dye. Smith, *First 100 Years in Cooke County,* 135.

61John M. Wiley was born in Tennessee in 1815 and moved to Texas in 1854. Landrum, *Grayson County, An Illustrated History of Grayson County, Texas,* 175.

62Isham Welch was born in Missouri in 1826 and moved to Grayson County, Texas, in 1856. *Ibid.,* 173.

63William Boyles was born in Kentucky in 1826 and migrated to Grayson County, Texas, prior to July 1, 1848, as a member of the Peters Colony. He is listed as a farmer in the 1850 federal census of Grayson County (family no. 14). Connor, *Peters Colony of Texas,* 198.

us to take our guns and go—myself and Ramey Dye. The reason we did not go to rescue Harper was because a messenger (Essman) told us that there were a great many soldiers in Gainesville and we were then afraid.

Gilbert Smith sworn.

[WITNESS.] I was at the meeting on Wednesday night. Present: Ramey Dye, James Powers, Moses Powers, John Ware, John W. Morris, Dr. Foster, H. J. Esman, Harry Gilman, Arphax Dawson, O. B. Atkinson, and Wm Boyles. We were all ordered to bring our guns. I loaded mine after I got there. I suppose there were twenty-eight men in all.

Our object was to come here, (Gainesville) and rescue the prisoners. Ramey Dye was chosen captain. We concluded to get away when Essman came and reported the number of men in town. We adjourned to meet again the next night and consult what to do. I understood we had spies out. Mr. Welch started up here to see how many men were in town. He was sent by the company. Some men were sent out two or three times to spy out and see if any body approached. Old Man Cochran went over to Red River to see how many members of the order there were over in that section. Snodgrass was there when I arrived. I understood that the signs would protect us when the Northern army came.

Dye was found guilty and hung.

[TRIAL OF D. M. LEFFEL]

The State vs. D M Leffel	Disloyalty & Treason

Leffel being arraigned before the Court, pleads guilty and says: "I was sworn by Wm Boyles, who gave me the signs, grip, and password. I was sworn to support the old Constitution and Union."

Leffel was connected with the Ramey Dye meeting for the rescue of the prisoners. He was found guilty and hung.

[TRIAL OF JAMES A. WARD AND W. B. TAYLOR]

The State vs. James A. Ward and W. B. Taylor	Disloyalty & Treason

On being arraigned before the Court [they] acknowledged their connection with the order—took the oath to support the old Constitution and Union. They gave the Court the signs, grip, and password.

Found guilty, and hung.

[TRIAL OF H. J. ESMAN]

The State vs. H. J. Esman	Disloyalty & Treason

Reference in this case is made to the trial of Ramey Dye. He was courier for Capt. Dye, and but for the bold manner in which he performed his wicked task, the Ramey Dye party would doubtless have been captured. He passed through the lines into Gainesville, unmolested, but dreading the risk of encountering the picket on his return, he waited till after dark; then he stripped himself of hat, coat, and boots and crawled a half mile, like the serpent, across the prairie; and escaped the notice of the picket.

Found guilty & hung.

[TRIAL OF W. W. JOHNSON]

THE STATE vs. W. W. JOHNSON	DISLOYALTY & TREASON

The prisoner confessed his connection with the order and gave the signs, grip, and [pass]word; took the oath to support the Old Constitution; was in the meeting at the Steam Mill, called for the purpose of rescuing Harper and others.

Found Guilty, & hung.

[TRIAL OF RICHARD N. MARTIN]

THE STATE
VS.
RICHARD N. MARTIN

DISLOYALTY &
TREASON

I. L. Ozment sworn.

[WITNESS.] R. N. Martin told me that there existed a secret organization in the Country; and if I would go with him, he could take me in an hour where I could learn all about it. I consented to go. He took me to the residence of Wm. Boyles; and after going a short distance from the house Boyles initiated me. He swore me to support the old Constitution and Union. He gave me the signs, grip and password.

Martin was found guilty and after being sentenced confessed his crimes. Upon the scaffold, in the presence of citizens and soldiers, he delivered the following address:

Gentlemen: When I first joined the secret organization, I did not fully understand its objects and intentions. But afterwards I received a document containing its plans. Although I am to die upon this tree, before I am hung I want to tell all I know concerning this order; and I desire it made known to the world.

You commenced the work to break up this secret order in good time. By this time it would have been too late for you. It was our intention to rise up and kill all southern men, women and children and take possession of their property. To the very best of my understanding this was the purpose.

Now, I pray that you will go on with this work, until every member of this order is brought to justice. I can refer you to one whom I desire shall be punished as I am punished; I want him hung to the same limb to which I am hung—my brother-in-law, Wm. Boyles. He is the author of my ruin. I took his counsel, and being a bad man, he gave me bad advice. (Here, he informed the people, where Boyles might be found.) Hunt him to the end of the world, or finish him, for his crimes. I hope I may be forgiven. Although I have injured the people so much I die with the consolation that in the end I done my duty to them.

Here his time expired and he was launched into eternity. Boyles [was later] killed at Collinsville.

[TRIAL OF BARNABAS BIRCH]

The State vs. Barnabas Birch[64]	Disloyalty & Treason

On being arraigned he confessed his guilt, giving the signs, grip, and password. He was a participant in the Ramey Dye meeting. While his trial was pending he addressed the court as follows:

One night recently I had a remarkable dream, which run this way: I thought that the North had overrun and surrounded the South which disheartened me. I could see no way for the South to escape. This dream, with what I heard (of the organization,) determined my course. I further dreamed that the Federals took me prisoner, and an officer gave me some liquor and I drank it; and it proved to be the best liquor I ever drank in my life.

Truly, 'the old men shall see visions, and the young men shall dream dreams.'

Birch was found guilty and hung.

---

[64]Barnabas Birch enlisted in the company of volunteers organized at Gainesville, May 23, 1861, by Captain W. C. Twitty. Smith, *First 100 Years in Cooke County*, 31.

[GROUP TRIAL]

The State vs. Curd Goss, Wm Anderson John Miller, Ar[phax] Dawson, and M. W. Morris.	Disloyalty & Treason.

These prisoners all acknowledged their guilt, giving the signs, grip, and password, and were active members of Capt Ramey Dye's company.

All found guilty and hung.

[TRIAL OF DR. JAMES FOSTER]

THE STATE vs. DR JAMES FOSTER (39)[65]	DISLOYALTY & TREASON

Dr. Foster, having been brought before the Court, was after trial ordered back to prison. While passing from the Court room to the prison, he attempted to escape and was shot by the guard. He lived only a few hours.

[65]Dr. James Foster was one of two physicians tried and condemned to death by the "Citizens Court." He emigrated to Texas from Missouri and was a resident of Grayson County in 1862.

[TRIAL OF A. N. JOHNSON AND JOHN COTTRELL]

THE STATE vs. A N JOHNSON, AND JOHN COTTRELL.	DISLOYALTY & TREASON.

The prisoners on being arraigned before the Court desired to be carried to Grayson County for trial. They were accordingly turned over to Capt. James D. Young, Com'g Company, Randolph's Battalion, Partizan Rangers.

Being members of this battalion, they were court martialed together, with Wm. McCool, who had been arrested on charges of treason, and all condemned and hung.

The history of Cottrell, is not a little diversified with adventure and romance. When the "Over Land Mail Route" was established in 1858, one of the employees, Mr Hawley, a genuine down-Easter, moved his family to Gainesville. His family consisted of Mrs Hawley and *her* daughter. These ladies were received in Society, and attracted no small degree of attention. They were evidently accomplished. Doubtless they were handsome, for both herself and daughter were distinguished by the enviable sobriquet, 'the beautiful Mrs Hawley and her pretty daughter.'

Soon after the breaking out of the war, Mr. Hawley fled the Country, going, no doubt, to his native home in the North. The lovely Mrs Hawley was left with no consolation but her wit, and no dowry but her beauty.

It was afterwards ascertained that she was left as a spy, and at the proper time she was to go to Missouri and, *perhaps* rejoin her husband. In the month of July 1862, (the pretty Miss Hawley, having united her destiny with a Mr Johnson in the holy bonds of wedlock,) Cottrell, Mrs Hawley, Johnson and his adored Armarylis set out for Missouri.

The citizens, thinking it unproper to give them a passport at that particular time, arrested their movements and lodged Cottrell and Johnson in prison.

Thus was spent the first night after marriage—the bridegroom in prison and the bride (only such, by virtue of the ceremony) weeping and blushing and wasting much sweetness on the desert air.

Again, just before the arrest of the prisoners on the 1st of Oct., Mrs Hawley attempted to escape north, taking the said Cottrell for her guide and help. This time she started east, sending out the information that she was going to Shreveport, La. How far she succeeded is partly explained by the following statement, of Mr Gilmore, of Gainesville:

> I called on an old friend of mine recently in Grayson County, sixteen miles east of Sherman. While there I was asked by the lady if I knew Dr. Cottrell of Gainesville. I told her that I knew a Mr. Cottrell, who was before the Provost Marshal when I saw him last. She then asked me if I knew Mrs. Cottrell, the widow of Mr Hawley, late of Gainesville. I told her that I knew Mrs. Hawley, but that she was not a widow, her husband having left our town on account of his Northern sentiments; and that Mrs. Hawley and Mr. Cottrell had gone to Shreveport.
>
> She then told me that not long since Cottrell called at her house and asked to stay several days with his family—that their youngest child was sick and the family very much fatigued. Mr Cottrell said that he had some business in the Indian Nation and wished them to stay until he returned. That night they demeaned themselves as man and wife, occupying the same room.
>
> Cottrell left the next morning. During the day, Mrs. Hawley took from her trunk a likeness of Dr Cottrell and asked one of the children if she [did] not love her good Papa. The lady of the house remarked that none of the children favored their father.
>
> Mrs Hawley replied that the Doctor was not the father of the children; that she was a widow, and the Doctor a widower; that her husband died in California and the Doctor's wife died in Missouri, and moved to Texas at the beginning of the war; and they were married about three months previous to that time. She said that as soon as times would permit, they intended to go to Missouri. All the children called Cottrell their good Papa. The Doctor did not return. I know the family who related this to me to be highly respectable and their statements worthy of credit.
>
> [signed] John T. Gilmore
>
> Sworn to and subscribed before the undersigned authority, this 19th day of October 1862, at office in Gainesville Texas
>
> Lemuel Gooding
> Clk C C. C. C.

This story of Cottrell and his wayward paramour was an ingenious fabrication, a lie from beginning to end. Cottrell had a wife in Cook [*sic*] County and Mrs Hawley a husband in the North. Cottrell only went to Red River to take observations and ascertain, if possible, the most eligible point for crossing the river and escaping detection. In this undertaking he was discovered and arrested; and consequently never had an opportunity to return to his *family*.

William McCool,[66] who was hung with Johnson and Cottrell, was the son-in-law of Henry Fields, who was hung early after the organization of the Court.

Mrs. McCool, the daughter of Fields, is a lady much esteemed for her modesty, beauty and virtuous refinement. She was attached to her husband by the strongest ties of affection. But a short time previous she had secretly abandoned her father's roof, to join her destiny to her bold and determined lover. How sad and melancholly [*sic*] the reflection that she who loved so well could not have loved more wisely. Or, why could he not, 'Taste the honey, and not wound the flower.'

A Mr Floyd who was arrested on the charge of being a member of the organization attempted to escape, and was fired upon and killed by the guard.

---

[66]William A. McCool enlisted in Captain W. C. Twitty's company of volunteers at Gainesville on May 23, 1861. *Ibid.*

[CONCLUSION]

We have now written what we designed to write concerning the proceedings of the "Citizens Court." The Jury as well as all others who were connected with the scenes of that day desired that all the evidence in each case should be published. It is to be regretted that it has not been done.

But it is the opinion of all that a complete transcript from the record of the Court would have been unnecessary to vindicate the course pursued, and would also have made a volume of too large a size for general public notice.

The evidence reveals a plot which, for its magnitude, infamy, treachery, and barbarity, is without a parallel in the annals of crime.

The testimony, while it has satisfied the public of the existence of an organized body of men associated together for the purpose of the overthrow of the government and the destruction of life and property, also justifies the citizens in the course they pursued in bringing the offenders to justice.

It is objected by some that the measures adopted by the citizens were rash, hasty, and unwarranted by any urgent necessity, contending justice would have been meeted [*sic*] out to the criminals in due time by due process of law. But we feel assured that those who make this objection have not been advised of the facts as they are now shown to the world.

But still, some will condemn the action of the citizens and jury; but it will be only those who sympathise with the conspirators and who would have given aid and comfort to their infamous designs. The guilt of the conspirators is questioned by none. That they deserved death is granted by all. To have given them time to have matured their plans for the accomplishment of their purposes would have condemned the citizens to eternal infamy. That their designs would very soon have culminated in open acts of violence, bloodshed, robbery and the most wanton licentiousness cannot be denied.

So imminent was the danger of an outbreak that it gave the detectives but little time to mature their plans to discover and round up the "Order."

It is owing to this fact that the full range of this widespread scheme was not ascertained, and more counties than Cook [*sic*] purged of conspirators and traitors.

After the arrests had been made, the prisoners confined to jail, it was ascertained that it was a fundamental element in the order, sustained by solemn oaths, to rescue its members from the authorities when arrested by them. To this information was added the alarming intelligence that meetings were being held at the hour of midnight, attended by many armed men, for the purpose of planning an attack upon Gainesville, and [of] rescuing the prisoners. One of those companies came within a few miles of town; but the prompt and efficient soldiery deterred them from their purpose.

In the mean time, intelligence had been received from adjoining counties that they were alarmingly infected with the same clan of desparadoes [*sic*].

The gallant sons of Cook [*sic*] being in the army, the county was almost destitute of sufficient strength to restore quiet and confidence. Something had to be done and the guilty had to be punished. The proceedings of the Citizens Court are characterized with as much wisdom, justice and moderation as may anywhere be found in the history of criminal procedure.

Out of sixty-eight cases brought before the Court, thirty-nine were condemned and hung and the others turned over to the Provost Marshal, or finally discharged from custody.

A careful examination of the testimony will show that many were implicated who were discharged, indicating the spirit that should prevail with all tribunals: that if error was [to be] committed, they desired it should be on the side of mercy.

DE LEMERON'S CASE.

It will be seen from the proceedings in this case, tried before the Dist. Court, that the proceedings of the citizens Jury conform to the rules prescribed by the Statutes and laws of the State in the trial of criminal causes before the organized Courts of Justice. It may be clearly seen that the Jury was governed by no testimony which was not held admissible under the strict and guarded rules of evidence [as] known [under] both statute and common law of the land. DeLemeron's case is considered a *mild case* when compared with those upon which the Jury acted.

The proceedings in the case of the State vs. DeLemeron are founded upon the charges contained in the following:

Bill of Indictment.

THE STATE OF TEXAS COUNTY OF COOK [*sic*]	IN THE DIST. COURT, FALL TERM, 1862.

In the name and by the authority of the State of Texas, the Grand Jurors for the County of Cook [*sic*], duly selected, empanelled, sworn and charged to inquire of offences committed in said County of Cook [*sic*] and State of Texas, upon their oaths present;

That on the 3rd day of November, in the year of our Lord, One Thousand Eight Hundred and Sixty Two, and long before and continually from thence, an open and public war was, and is yet prosecuted and carried on between the United States of America and the Confederate States of America, our said State of Texas being one of said Confederate States;

to-wit: in the County of Cook [*sic*] and State aforesaid, that one Joel Francis DeLemeron, a citizen of our said County and State aforesaid, then and there, well-knowing the premises but not regarding the duty of his allegiance, nor having the fear of God in his heart; and being moved and seduced by the instigations of the Devil, as a false traitor to and against our said State, and wholly withdrawing his allegiance, fidelity and obedience, which every true and faithful citizen of our said State should and of right ought to bear toward our said State, and contriving, and with all his strength intending, to aid and assist the said United States, so being an enemy to our said State, as aforesaid, in the prosecution of said war against our said State of Texas,

to wit: On the third day of November and in the year aforesaid, and on numerous other days, before as well as after, with force and arms in the County and State aforesaid, maliciously and traitorously was adhering to, and aiding and comforting the said United States, being then an enemy to our said State as aforesaid; and that in the prosecution and performance of his treason and traitorous adherings as aforesaid, he, the said Joel Francis DeLemeron, was such traitor as aforesaid during the said war; to wit: On the day and year aforesaid, and on many other days, did then and there materially aid the said enemy, and adhere to the same, by consulting, advising, and bearing information, with and to them, the said United States by entering into secret, vile, traiterous [*sic*] and treasonable associations for the overthrow of our said State, and for the destruction of the lives and property of the good citizens, thereof, by drilling, directing and instructing the aforesaid enemy with arts of war,

to wit: in the use of fire arms and other implements of war.

And further in the prosecution, performance and execution of his treasonable and traitorous adherings as aforesaid, the said Joel Francis DeLemeron, afterwards and during the said war;

to wit: On the third day of November in the year aforesaid and on divers other days in the County and State aforesaid did adhere to the said enemy of our said State and give them aid and comfort by furnishing said enemy, the United States of America; to wit: horses, bridles, saddles, blankets, guns, ammunition and provisions in large numbers and quantities, and of great value.

The above charged treasonable and traitorous acts are special overt acts of adhering to, aiding and comforting the enemy aforesaid, and are specially so charged, contrary to the Constitution and the Statute in such cases made and provided, and against the peace and dignity of our said State of Texas

Daniel Montague
Foreman, Grand Jury.

W. H. Andrews,
Dist. Attorney.
20th Judicial Dist.
State of Texas.

Testimony

Dr. George Bradley sworn.

[Witness.] On the 30th day of Oct. 1862, I went to the house of Joel F. De Lemeron, residing in Cook [*sic*] County Texas, for the purpose of ascertaining the whereabouts of two gentlemen, Ware and Boyles. I found Mr. De Lemeron, his wife and another lady in the house. I told them that my name was Miller, brother to the Miller who was executed at Gainesville; and that I was laying a plan to avenge his death.

I told them I had one hundred men in Den. Hollow, and was there trying to find a man by the name of Ware, with his men, as it was my intention to burn Gainesville on Saturday night and take the principal men who were engaged in the execution of my friends.

He then directed me by a secret path to Mr Ware's house but said it was almost impossible for me to get round Mr. Dister's, his nearest neighbor. I then asked him some questions about Mr. Dister's wealth and his horses. He answered that he was rich and had good horses. His wife requested that I should not take any of his horses, as he was a good neighbor.

De Lemeron said no, that he was French; and Dister [was] Dutch, and they had nothing to do with this family quarrel—that they were *neutrals.* His wife wished me great success and said her husband could do so, too, if he were not afraid. De Lemeron said that he had to *lie low* and say nothing.

He said he had gone to Mrs. Ware's contrary to orders from Southern men, and had repaired her wagon—that he had loaned Mrs. Boyles his horse under the cloak of being hired from the old widow lady living with him, and that he intended to assist them. (Ware and Boyles belonged to the clan, and had ran [*sic*] away, and DeLemeron was assisting their families to get to Missouri).

I then got some men to go with me to Bluff Springs in search of Ware and Boyles. We went to De Lemeron's house that night between midnight and day. He opposed the course of the Southern men in Cook [*sic*] County in bitter language. But he said he had to *lie low* and say nothing; for if a man lived in Rome, he had to do as Romans done: and as he lived in Texas, he had to do, as Texans done. I then remarked to them all that I did not believe DeLemeron would inform on us. He said he would not. His wife then said, "If the truth must come, my husband is as good a Union man as I am a woman—and I am as good as they ever make 'em."

De Lemeron said that he was not so *stuck* with southern men as to obey all calls. When I left, he told me to call at any hour of the night, and I should have what information and provisions I wanted; and if I saw Ware, to tell him he need not be afraid to come to his house at any time, for information or provisions.

On the 31st of Oct. 1862, I went to see John Wisdom and told him what had transpired, and to get some men; and if I possibly could, I would meet him at Mr. Strouds that night. If I could not, for him to go on and sound the Frenchman on his northern principles. On the 1st November, 1862, I met De Lemeron at Mr. Robinson's in company with Messrs Stroud and Wisdom. De Lemeron took me to one side and asked me if that man (pointing to Wisdom) was one of my party. I told him he was. He then said that Wisdom came to his house and represented himself as such, but he thought he might be a Gainesville spy and would give him (Wisdom) no satisfaction. Upon which he took him, De Lemeron, prisoner, for fear he (De Lemeron) would betray him, (Wisdom).

I told him, he might consider him released, as those men were true and faithful Union men.

Wisdom told De Lemeron that he had a company and some of his men had no arms, and he desired to get some guns. De Lemeron at once offered his gun, shot pouches and ammunition. He then said, that he, with twenty or twenty-five of his neighbors at the head of Elm, were ready last summer to join the order, but no one had ever mentioned it to them—that they were all strong Union men and spoke of coming down in this country to join, as they had heard such a party spoken of. He then said he was willing to go with us to Gainesville and burn it, and take the principal men prisoners, and commit any deprivations we thought advisable.

He spoke of being a good drill officer. I told him he was the very man I wanted, as I was ignorant of military matters. He desired, if we gave any offices, to get the Adjutant's place. Wisdom and myself promised him that office in our Regt. It was then suggested that we should drill some before going into action. Upon which De Lemeron proposed to meet us at Mr. Stroud's spring on Sunday night, and for Wisdom and myself to bring our lieutenants, and first seargeants [*sic*], as they would be sufficient.

We met at the time and place appointed and received instructions in the arts of war from De Lemeron. He then proposed to muster what strength we could and make our way to the Northern army, then stationed on the North Fork of the Canadian River. He proposed further to go by where Capt. Garrison was, with his men, and if we deemed our united strength sufficient, we would return and avenge our wrongs. If not, pursue our course to the Northern army.

We then agreed to meet again the next night. We met and De Lemeron told me he had purchased two horses from Mr. York, to be paid for in Cook [*sic*] County, or State, scrip—that he had borrowed a gun from Mr. Dister under the pretense of guarding the Gainesville and Pilot Point road that night.

De Lemeron's advice was to take every man prisoner we met, to go by Col. Bourland's, and if he should be willing, take him along; if not, we will shoot him. I then administered to him the oath to support the Constitution and government of the United States. It was then proposed to drill again, as Capt. Shannon (Wisdom) had not arrived. He then drilled us about two hours.

I then informed him that my name was Bradly, instead of Miller; that I was a southern man, and so were all my men, and that I intended to carry him to Gainesville to be tried before the District Court then in session.

Robt. Wheelock sworn.

[Witness.] I met the prisoner at the bar on the 30th day of Oct. last, at Stroud's spring in this County, to lay plans (as he said) for crossing Red River. I was introduced to him as a friend of De Lemeron. He said we must join Capt. Garrison and organize; and if strong enough, to fall upon Texas and go fighting and take what we wanted. He said go by Col. Bourland's, and if we could not make him go with us, he would shoot him down and leave him kicking. Dr. Bradly administered to him the oath to support the old constitution and Union.

He brought with him two horses and one gun, which he exultingly said he had bought from York and paid him in Quartermaster's receipts. He said he could find Capt. Garrison in two or three days; that he was below Bourlands' [bend], on this or the other side of the River.

George Dister sworn.

QUESTION. Do you know the prisoner at the bar?

ANS. I do.

QUESTION. Where did you see him last before meeting him here?

ANS. At his own house, on the 3rd day of Nov. last. He was saddling two ponies and said he had been appointed picket guard on the Gainesville and Pilot Point Road. He asked me for a rifle gun and promised to return it the next morning.

QUESTION. Did he return the gun.

ANS. No; the men who had him in custody returned it to me.

A. H. York sworn.

[WITNESS.] I sold two horses to De Lemeron on the 3d day of Nov. last. He told me he was appointed agent by Genl. Hudson to buy property for the government. He promised to come to Gainesville and get a Quartermaster's receipt for the amount the horses were valued at.

J. L. Wisdom sworn.

[WITNESS.] De Lemeron told me that after perfecting an organization with Capt. Garrison's men, we would then come back to Gainesville and take it, as it would be a light job—that the plunder of the town was ours already.

Geo. C. Wright sworn.

[WITNESS.] On the night of the first of Oct. 1862, I went down to the Dripping Springs as a scout for the Command at Gainesville. I met Capt. Garrison at the head of a company of armed men. He halted me and said: "Who comes there?" I answered: "Wright," and repeated his inquiry: adding, "is that Capt. Garrison?" He answered in the affirmative and asked what I wanted. I told him I was a police-man, and he knew my business. "Well," said he, "if that is your business here, you had better leave. We have wronged no person or property.

So I want you to leave, and if you desire to get away, you had better go quick." I did leave quickly and reported to the commander at Gainesville.

S. A. Blain sworn.

[WITNESS.] There are persons at large in the vicinity of Red River where Capt. Garrison is reported to be by the prisoner at the bar. Southern men have been ambuscaded and fired upon by them. I have seen such persons; was nearby, in sight, when they fired upon and killed Col. Wm. C. Young of this county. At that time we were hunting the body of James Dixon, who had previously been killed by such persons.

Judge Waddell's Charge to the Jury.

THE STATE OF TEXAS VS. JOEL FRANCIS DE LEMERON	FOR TREASON

The constitution of the State of Texas defines treason thus: "Treason against the State of Texas shall consist in levying war against it, in adhering to its enemies, giving them aid and comfort."

The Indictment charges; "that on the 3rd day of November, 1862, the accused committed treason against the State of Texas, in the County of Cook [*sic*], by then and there adhering to our enemies, the United States of North America, and furnishing them horses, bridles, saddles, blankets, guns, and ammunition in large quantities, and of great value."

It further charges; "that he then and there joined a treasonable association for the overthrow of the State of Texas." A mere conspiracy, or intention to adhere to the enemy, is not treason—actual adherence must be proved. The Jury will weigh well the evidence in this case, and must be satisfied that the association into which he was sworn was treasonable, and for the overthrow of our State, and that the accused entered it well-knowing that the object of the conspiracy was treasonable, and that he entered it voluntarily, and not by compulsion. The evidence must further satisfy the Jury that the accused actually adhered to our enemies, the United States, and did furnish them the articles specified above, at the time and place specified in the Indictment; and with a traitorous intent. And if you should so believe, from the evidence, you will find him guilty of treason; and if you so find, you will in your verdict also say whether the punishment shall be death, or confinement in the penitentiary for life. If the Jury believe from the evidence that the accused had voluntarily determined to betray the State of Texas, and attempted to get to the enemy with the articles as charged in the Indictment, and was arrested, and by that arrest was prevented from reaching the enemy, he is as guilty as if he had reached the enemy's lines. The citizens of Texas have the legal right to disguise themselves as the enemies of the country in order to discover the treasonable machination of those whom they may regard as untrue to our government, and it is also, their duty to take such lawful steps. If upon a survey of all the evidence in the case, the Jury have a reasonable doubt as to the guilt of the accused, it is their duty to acquit—the law established maxim being; "it is better that ninety and nine guilty men should escape, than that one innocent man should suffer."

R. S. Waddell,
Dist. Judge

Verdict of the Jury

We, the Jury, find the Defendant guilty, and assess his punishment—confinement in the Penitentiary for life.

I A Moore
Foreman

Having thus ended our notice of the criminal proceedings against the Conspirators, we will refer to some of the consequences of this wicked conspiracy, against the peace of the State and the lives of its citizens.

Our eyes are at first met by scenes of horror and bloodshed; the commission of crimes unexampled and unsurpassed in the annals of atrocities performed through human agents, make up the record of this organization.

In our first glance at its melancholly [*sic*] results, our hearts at once entwine around the memory of the brave, the generous and lamented Col. Young, who fell at the hands of those who fed at his barn yard and eat at his table.

We are called upon to morn the death of that noble and useful citizen, James Dixon. We are called to view the horrible deeds of the merciless savage, led on and inspirited in his insatiable thirst for blood by those whom we blindly called friends and patriots. We are called upon to record the death of Bicknell and others at Fort Cobb—the destruction of property and the indiscriminate slaughter, and almost entire extermination of the Tankaway [*sic*] tribe of Indians; the only tribe of the "Reserves" true and loyal to the South.

DEATH OF JAMES DIXON.[67]

The first victim of this infamous plot was James Dixon. Mr. Dixon was a quiet and peaceable citizen and had taken little or no part in the arrest and trial of the members of the order. After the general arrest had been made, and pending the trial of the prisoners, Mr. Dixon visited his friend on Red River. It was soon proposed to go hunting. When they had reached the river bottom, they discovered a man in the edge of the timber, whose strange conduct attracted their attention. They approached the swamp and (the man having concealed himself) began a search.

Immediately they were fired upon by a body of men in ambush, and Dixon fell from his horse, mortally wounded.

His friend made his escape, and soon obtained sufficient strength to recover the body of Dixon. When he returned with his neighbors, Dixon was dead. He had evidently received some attention at the hands of his murderers—perhaps died under the sting of their insults and wicked menaces and execrations.

He had been removed from the spot where he fell and placed in the shade of a swamp oak, his hat placed over his face; and other circumstances plainly indicated the presence of the murderers at the site of the dying man.

His wife, so highly esteemed for her many virtues and exemplary and Christian character, became a prey to inconsolable grief and died with a broken heart soon after the murder of her husband.

Death of Col Young[68]

[67]James [M.?] Dixon was born in North Carolina in 1826 and migrated after 1850 to Cooke County, Texas, by way of Missouri. U. S. Eighth Census, 1860 (Returns of Schedule 1, Free Inhabitants, for Cooke County, Texas, microfilm, Dallas Public Library), family no. 32.

[68]With this heading on the last extant page of his manuscript, George W. Diamond indicated his intention to include a recapitulation of the circumstances of the death of W. C. Young, as he had of the death of James Dixon. If Diamond wrote such an addendum, it has not been discovered among his papers, or elsewhere.

Afterword

By L. D. Clark

From the time when I began to comprehend the talk of grown-ups, I took in the horror of the Great Hanging and shivered in thinking of it. My great-grandfather, Nathaniel Miles Clark, was one of the victims. We lived close to where he and his family settled on coming to Texas in 1857, seven miles southeast of Gainesville. What we knew about the atrocity had been passed on largely by my grandfather James Lemuel Clark, who lived until 1932 and talked a great deal about it. I was ten years old when he died.

Back then we knew of no surviving records of the trials. Few relatives of either victims or perpetrators went on living in the region after the event was over with and the Civil War ended. Descendants were reluctant to bring up the subject, an attitude also prevalent among the general public around Gainesville: the Great Hanging was a terrible scandal that "we just don't talk about." My family did not share this hesitation. We never forgot the merciless injustice of it all. Comments and condemnations circulated at large through our extended family discourse: not against descendants of the perpetrators, a few of whom we knew, for we harbored no continuing enmities with the living. Our talk was in fierce denunciations by Pappy and his brothers, and by Grandpa Clark, of the vigilante court through which the mob, aided and abetted by the Confederate military under Colonel James Bourland, hanged more than forty Unionists in Gainesville in October 1862.

We should remember, as background, that Cooke County voted two-to-one against secession in the statewide referendum in 1861, and a deep hostility between Unionists and secessionists simmered on after the war broke out, ready to surface and explode when conflict arose over Confederate military conscription, passed into law with exemptions for large slaveholders: which in turn led to formation of a secret resistance movement of Unionists against the Confederacy, whose chief aim was to restore the Union, even to the point of undertaking or participating in military action when the time seemed ripe. Grandpa Clark decided in his seventies to write up his recollections of the Civil War. He was serving against his will in the Confederate army, and was campaigning against the Union in Missouri at the very time his father was lynched.

When he heard of this he deserted and came home and managed to stay in Cooke County to take care of his widowed mother and his several younger siblings by enlisting in a frontier ranger unit whose duty was to protect settlers from Indians. Ironically, it was commanded by Colonel James Bourland. A year later, after actual bloodshed between Unionists and Confederates in Bourland's very outfit, he found he must join a refugee flight to the North. All this he recounts in *Civil War Recollections of James Lemuel Clark.* The manuscript of these memoirs lay in a trunk for years before I learned of them; early on we did not have even these to assist our memory when we spoke of the Great Hanging.

I remember full well, though, the first written account that came our way: it was a facsimile of Thomas Barrett's *The Great Hanging at Gainesville,* published by the author in 1885. We knew of him as a member of the so-called citizens' court, and we laced into his memory often enough as one of the murderers of Nathaniel Miles, but we were not aware that he had ever written a defense of his motives and actions. Our minister, Brother Chisum, who was acquainted with the fate of Nathaniel Miles, told Pappy one day about having come across Barrett's account. This was a welcome jolt to us, the first we knew that anything had ever been written down about the ghastly affair. What Brother Chisum had was a reproduction of Barrett's book done in the purplish typography of the old-fashioned ditto machine by some librarian. He lent it to us for a while and we read it but took no steps to make a copy of our own. This piece of luck came our way not long after Grandpa Clark died. The next I heard of Barrett's book, in the 1950s, it was as one of the rarest items of Texana. Sometime around this time a copy came into the hands of the Texas State Historical Association, which published it in pamphlet form in 1961. But this went out of print at least twenty years ago.

Now we should bear in mind that Barrett's is one of only two contemporary accounts of the Great Hanging, and the only one from an eyewitness. The other, by George Washington Diamond, based on transcriptions of the proceedings of the kangaroo court, lay unknown for over a century before being published. The *Southwestern Historical Quarterly* brought it out in 1963. This edition was not available for long either, so for the many years up to now no one has been able to study this significant event in Texas Civil War history except in secondary sources.

Barrett's account repeatedly makes clear what a murderous farce the whole affair of the Great Hanging was. When he was ordered to come to Gainesville on the morning of October 1, 1862, and arrived to find more than a hundred Unionists had been rounded up and imprisoned, the mob with the Confederate military behind it was already in control:

talk of lynching was flying around and a giant elm on Pecan Creek had already been selected for the stringing up. Martial law was in force, with Colonel James Bourland as provost marshal, which meant he could get away with almost anything—and in ruthless fashion he did. All choices being ultimately his, he allowed and often directed going back and forth among the vigilante jury and court martial and brazen lynching by the mob. The formation of the so-called jury was a renegade proceeding from the outset. Colonel William Young was voted in as chairman by the mob. In a great show of fairness he appointed a committee of five men, who in turn selected a jury of twelve—seven of whom just happened, of course, to be slaveholders, and it was decided they would convict or acquit by majority vote. Diamond goes so far as to maintain that the set-up must have been commendable because the finest men in the county were behind it: a man of fine reputation can do no wrong, an argument best left to the foolish. (Later visitors who approved of the process would argue that it must have been defensible if a minister and doctor like Thomas Barrett participated: a backhand compliment that he found insulting.)

The jury selection was actually no more than a pyramid proceeding decorated with a show-trial legality that deceived only those who wanted to be deceived. We can know what a matter of fraudulent justice it was in how it spurned the due process of law to which every American is entitled, and as we may suppose, every dweller in the Confederacy as well. The worst pretense of all was charging the accused, guilty only of conspiracy, with committing crimes intended by a few, constantly mentioned as the murder of women and children, none of which was ever committed by anyone. What occurred in Grayson County places the reign of terror in Cooke County precisely where it belongs. A vigilante tribunal was considered in Sherman for sixteen accused conspirators, but wiser heads prevailed: the defendants were remanded to a district court in Tyler, where they were all acquitted or released on bail from which they never returned, and no one felt it necessary to go after them. Contrast the character of the Gainesville vigilante court as described in a letter to Thomas Barrett from P. T. Andrews, the only other eyewitness whose report we have. He was visiting Barrett in 1862 from Grayson County, where he later became County Judge, he sat in on "Citizens' Court" sessions and called the jury a "blood-thirsty body," and witnessed that in Grayson County "we did not have such bloodthirsty spirits as you had in Cooke."

I remember well my first contact with the Diamond treatment. My father-in-law, a subscriber to the *Southwestern Historical Quarterly*, showed me the issue in which the defense appeared, saying that I must know something about the Great Hanging, since it took place in my hometown; he himself had never heard of it.

I think I went a little dizzy on hearing this. Here was a second contemporary document concerning the old atrocity that had lain concealed for a hundred years. How this had happened took a little while to understand. George Washington Diamond was a newspaperman serving in the Confederate army, and although not present during the trials, he was asked by the instigators, who turned all court records over to him, to draw up a justification of their blanket prosecution of Unionists. They must have felt that whoever won the war, the law might be looking into the legitimacy of what they had done. This did happen, in that Bourland and all members of the vigilante court were indicted for murder by restored state authority under the Union, but by incredible blundering most of the dispensation of justice ended up in the hands of former Confederates after all and no punishment was ever meted out to anyone. Eventually these cases, along with many other instances of Confederate barbarity, were wiped clean by the general amnesty issued by the Federal government for crimes committed under Confederate jurisdiction. This was a cruel blow to Unionists, who had hotly anticipated legal vengeance against those who persecuted and murdered members of their families during the insurrection. But then one must admit that general amnesty probably did prevent a balkanization of Texas, or for that matter of the whole South.

It is not clear when George Washington Diamond began writing his planned vindication of the kangaroo court: it seems not to have been anytime during the remaining years of the conflict, nor in the turmoil just following the end of it. No public influence of his account is evident at any time. Just when he began writing it as it stands in the *Southwestern Historical Quarterly* and in this volume is difficult to establish. In his own words on an early page he speaks of the court records as if they were fully assembled when the trials ended, endorsed by the members of the court and delivered to him to publish in the exact approved form at his discretion. This is obviously not what happened. Diamond confirms that sixty-eight cases were tried by the court. The testimony of the accused and the charges leveled by the prosecution, as taken down by two court reporters, must have been voluminous. Diamond picks and chooses, quite plainly, but tries to leave the impression that he is not doing so. For instance, he never brings up cases in which defendants were acquitted, only those which saw them convicted, often with sentences handed down and questionable confessions intoned in bombast. At times he turned to outright misrepresentation, one of the most outrageous of which was to conceal behind the term "group trial" the mob seizure of fourteen men for lynching against whom charges were scheduled to be dropped. The mob hanged them all during the next two days, under protection of a military escort furnished by Bourland. The account does not detail the retrials after the assassination of Colonel Young of the last nineteen men lynched on no sane charges at all, condemned by a jury from which three reasonable members had been dropped and were replaced by known seekers of vengeance against Unionists. By this time the whole madness had degenerated into show trials inflicted to rid the land of the political enemies of Bourland and his cohorts.

Again, Diamond was so deluded by his own pretensions that he failed to see how he marred his defense in his summing up of a trial in the regular term of district court about a month after the Great Hanging. He harped on this case as proof that the "citizens court" was perfectly legal. It was in fact a process identical to the practices of the kangaroo court, despite the said legality of it. This time a recent immigrant named DeLemeron wished to go north and join the Union war effort, but nothing that he planned, including delivery of horses and arms to Union forces, and the kidnapping or killing of Colonel Bourland, was ever carried out.He was lured into what he talked of by Confederate spies from Gainesville, who arrested and charged him with treason before he committed any. Worse, the foreman of the grand jury was none other than Daniel Montague, who had been "president" of the Great Hanging court. It did not hamper the DeLemeron jury that although District Judge Waddell in his instructions all but told them that the prosecution had no case. They convicted DeLemeron anyhow, and also sentenced him to hang, but the judge, though a secessionist, commuted the sentence to life imprisonment. In other words, the prosecution held to the same travesty of justice that the lynching jury had, only this time it was stopped short of the death penalty by a due-process judge.

We cannot tell how long Diamond labored over his manuscript. Internal evidence shows that he completed it between early 1874 and late 1876. His avowed purpose for writing is plainly sincere: he intends now, more than a decade after the horrendous episode, to justify the trials as regrettable but laudable duties of civic responsibility carried out by the best men in the community. Why he did not go ahead and publish what he had been so preoccupied with is a question seemingly never to be resolved. He did feel that he had finished his declared task, having "ended our notice of the criminal proceedings against the Conspirators." He felt called upon now, however, to magnify his allegations immensely:

to "make up the record of this organization" by charging it with "the commission of crimes unexampled and unsurpassed in the annals of atrocities performed through human agents," these to be wreaked by murderous Unionists allied with marauding Indians. The overblown rhetoric alone is enough to unmask the ridiculous claims. The first of these horrors unexampled in history had been the murder of James Dixon and Colonel William Young, to which he was about to turn when he wrote the "Death of Col Young" as the last surviving line of his manuscript.

We cannot know why Diamond changed his mind about expanding on the assassination of Colonel Young. Perhaps the mendacity of his own rhetoric glimmered alive in his mind insinuating that he had nothing more to say except what he had already puffed up into falsehood numerous times, and even he could not hallucinate other crimes that had never been committed. As for publication, we have no clue as to why he held back on immediate presentation of his completed effort to the public to ostensibly prove his case. A decade later he would have had good reason to pause. The Barrett book appeared, and since it came out and was circulated from within a few miles of where Diamond lived, he probably saw it. If so, it would have been a hard matter to defend his distorted report against the frankness and honesty of an eyewitness and participant. Maybe in leaving his manuscript with his descendants he indicated that they should publish it if ever this seemed appropriate.

Diamond was guilty, in whatever case, of one transgression against the spirit of history. While he took particular care to safeguard his own account of the Great Hanging trials, he took none at all to preserve the original records. It is plain from the tone and implication of his account that he feels all this testimony is of no further use to anyone, that he has recorded every word of it essential to history. This in itself leads us to suspect duplicity in laying out an agenda, and he even admits leaving out what he thought repetitious, such as when the testimony of one defendant seemed to coincide with that of another: a violation of the rules of evidence, to say the least. The assertions over and over that these members of the resistance planned a murderous rampage slaying women and children and seizing property as they went is borne out by the testimony of a few. So is admitting to espionage for the Union army, and so is a running on to congratulate the court for breaking up the resistance, almost to the point of a defendant agreeing with the jury that he ought to be hanged. All these leave a wealth of suspicion, and of coerced confessions, as do especially the much-repeated phrases that the condemned men confessed their crimes at the gallows, without his naming what the crimes were. All that the whole body of the accused could ever have been convicted of in a legitimate court of law was conspiracy against the Confederacy.

After Diamond died in 1911, more than one person searched for the original transcripts, going by hardly more than hints and guesses as to their whereabouts. The endeavor that I am best acquainted with dates from 1925, when Lillian Gunter of Gainesville contacted several possible leads inquiring into what happened to the transcripts. I have a copy of a letter informing her that they were last known to be in the hands of one Adam Hornback, who lived in Duck Creek, just north of Denison. Unhappily Miss Gunter died soon after she received the letter, before she could follow up, I imagine. Adam Hornback himself died in 1928. I have attempted to track down descendants and made other enquiries as to the fate of these precious documents, but all in vain. It appears that the original records of the Great Hanging, abandoned to chance by Diamond after he made his own prejudiced use of them are lost forever.

In the meantime, Diamond's own manuscript lay in the possession of his descendants, all the while unknown to history. At the end of a century it was in the hands of a granddaughter of his, Mrs. Harry Harlan. She is to be warmly thanked in that during celebration of the Civil War centennial she got in touch with the Texas State Historical Association and turned the manuscript over to them. They eagerly assigned two editors to prepare it for the publication it saw in the *Southwestern Historical Quarterly.* That it and the Barrett account will now be available in the present volume is once again owing to the generosity and historical astuteness of the said association.

Headstone of Nathaniel Miles Clark, near Gainesville, Texas. *Photo by Glen Sample Ely.*